BROOKLANDS COLLEGE LIBRARY
HEATH ROAD, WEYBRIDGE, SURREY KT13 8TT
Tel: (01932) 797906

This item must be returned on or before the last date
entered below. Subject to certain conditions, the loan
period may be extended upon application to the Librarian

D0513345

18. MAY 2005	18. JAN. 2007	03 FEB 2011
-7. JUN. 2005	-1. FEB. 2007	9 JAN 2012
2. SEP. 20..	19 FEB 2007	2 8 FEB 2012
31. OCT. 2005		
12. DEC. 2005		-6 MAR 2013
24. APR. 2006	8 JAN 2008	
17. MAY 2006	1 2 FEB 2008	27 MAR 2013
-6. OCT. 2006	1 3 MAY 2008	17 APR 2013
19. OCT. 2006	3rd June 08	0 8 MAY 2013
14. NOV. 2006	24 Jun 2008	
-7. DEC. 2006	- 6 NOV 2008	

Brooklands College Library WITHDRAWN FROM STOCK

AUTHOR JEFFCOATE

TITLE The new Sugarcraft course

CLASSIFICATION NO. 641.8653 - JEF

ACCESSION NO. 093887

BROOKLANDS COLLEGE LIBRARY
093887

The New
SUGARCRAFT
COURSE

The New
SUGARCRAFT
COURSE

CHRIS JEFFCOATE & JACKIE KUFLIK

MEREHURST

Dedication

Chris and Jackie would like to thank Doris and Gladys,
without whom this book would not have been written.
This book is dedicated to our children, with our love.

First published 1997 by Merehurst Limited
Ferry House, 51–57 Lacy Road, Putney,
London SW15 1PR

Copyright © Merehurst Limited 1997
ISBN 1-85391-655-X

All rights reserved. No part of this publication may be
reproduced, stored in a retrieval system or transmitted in
any form or by any means, electronic, mechanical,
photocopying, recording or otherwise, without prior written
permission of the copyright owner.

A catalogue record for this book is available from the
British Library.

Editor: Helen Southall
Design: Anita Ruddell
Photography by Clive Streeter

Colour separation by Bright Arts, Hong Kong
Printed in Italy by L.E.G.O.

CONTENTS

INTRODUCTION

Cake decorating skills and the art of sugarcraft continue to develop. With the introduction of the Creative Studies qualifications in sugarcraft, sugar has grown into an artform which, for the foreseeable future, knows no bounds.

This book outlines the knowledge required for a basic understanding of sugarcraft, and forms a starting point for anyone about to take up sugarcraft as a hobby or to embark on a course of study. Armed with the basics, we hope readers of this book will develop their skills, apply their own creativity, and continue to advance the amazing medium of sugar.

Jackie Murphie.

Chris Jeffcoate

BAKING

When making a cake on which you will spend a great deal of time decorating the outside, it is important to remember that the inside should be good as well. Although the first impression of any celebration cake is a visual one, the lasting impression is of its flavour, texture and eating quality. Your attention to these details will ensure that your cake is remembered as much for the pleasure of eating it as for its spectacular appearance.

CAKE TINS

A wide variety of tins is now available for cake baking. Tins are not only designed to be a particular shape and size; consideration is also given to ease of use and how the baked cake will be removed from the tin. Nevertheless, you should ensure that tins are well prepared.

VICTORIA SANDWICH (SHALLOW) TINS These are usually used in pairs. Place one tin on a double sheet of greaseproof paper, draw round the base with a pencil, and then cut out the discs of paper just inside the pencil line (to allow for the thickness of the tins). Grease the tins with vegetable fat (shortening), and fit one of the discs of paper into the bottom of each of the tins, then grease the paper to aid easy release of the sponge cakes. Use this method for Swiss roll tins as well (page 10).

DEEP CAKE TINS Measure the circumference of the cake tin first, using string or a tape measure. Cut a greaseproof paper strip, 5cm (2 inches) deeper than the tin and 5cm (2 inches) longer than the measured circumference. Fold up 2.5cm (1 inch) of the paper along one long edge, press to make a crease in the paper, then unfold. Grease the tin with vegetable fat (shortening). If

you are lining a tin with curved sides, snip with scissors along the folded edge up to the crease. This will help you fit the paper neatly around the edge of the tin. For straight-sided tins, you need only snip the folded area when fitting around corners. Fit the strip into position around the inside of the tin. Place the tin on a piece of greaseproof paper, draw around the base with a pencil, and cut out the shape just inside the pencil line. Fit the shape in the bottom of the tin so that it covers the snipped edges of the side lining paper.

Cakes that take a relatively long time to bake, especially rich fruit cakes, need some protection to ensure even baking. To achieve this, wrap a few layers of brown paper around the outside of the tin and fix into position with string.

MOULDED NOVELTY TINS These cannot be lined with paper so to

EXPERT ADVICE

Shiny new tins can reflect the heat, producing an uneven bake, so although you should wash tins after use, there is no need to remove the heat and baking marks.

ensure that your cake will not stick, first grease well with vegetable fat (shortening), and then dust liberally with plain flour. Knock out any excess flour before filling the tin with mixture.

If you are baking a large quantity of shaped cakes, or bake novelty cakes regularly, then a convenient method is to mix together equal amounts of vegetable fat and flour, and to brush this inside the tins. This mixture can be kept in the refrigerator in a sealed container, but bring it back to room temperature before using again.

BASIC CAKE RECIPES

Victoria Sandwich

MAKES ONE 18CM (7 INCH) SANDWICH CAKE

175g (6oz/ ¾ cup) butter, softened
175g (6oz/ ¾ cup) caster sugar
3 eggs (at room temperature), beaten
175g (6oz/1½ cups) self-raising flour
TO FINISH
Jam
Icing (confectioners') sugar

1 Grease and line the bases of two 18cm (7 inch) sandwich tins (page 8). Preheat the oven to 180°C (350°F/Gas 4).

2 Cream together the butter and sugar until it is light and fluffy. Add the beaten egg in three stages, beating well after each addition. If the mixture starts to curdle, add a spoonful of flour with each addition of egg.

3 Sift the flour on to the mixture, and fold in gently with a large metal tablespoon or your hand.

4 Divide the mixture between the prepared tins, and bake in the oven for approximately 20 minutes or until the tops of the cakes are firm when pressed with your fingertips. The cake should spring back to shape and the fingermarks disappear.

5 Turn the cakes out of the tins on to a wire rack. Peel off the lining paper, and leave the cakes to cool.

6 When the cakes are cool, sandwich them together with jam. Place a paper doily on top, dust with icing sugar, then carefully remove the doily, for a simple but effective decoration.

VARIATIONS

CHOCOLATE Replace 1 tablespoon flour with 1 tablespoon cocoa powder, and add 1 tablespoon milk.

COFFEE Dissolve instant coffee granules in a little boiling water to make a strong solution. The amount you use depends on taste, but 1 teaspoon granules mixed with 2 teaspoons water is a good guide. Add to the mixture after adding the egg.

ORANGE Add the grated zest of 1 orange when beating in the eggs.

LEMON Add the grated zest of 1 lemon when beating in the eggs.

VANILLA Beat in 2 teaspoons vanilla essence with the eggs.

EXPERT ADVICE

When mixing a cake, curdling usually occurs because the ingredients are too cold. Make sure you start with everything at room temperature.

Boiled Chocolate Cake

MAKES ONE 18CM (7 INCH) ROUND CAKE

100g (4oz/ ½ cup) margarine
100g (4oz/ ⅓ cup) black treacle
100g (4oz/ ⅓ cup) golden syrup
50g (2oz/ ⅓ cup) brown sugar
150ml (¼ pint/ ⅔ cup) milk
2 eggs
200g (7oz/1 ¾ cups) plain flour
25g (1oz/ ¼ cup) cocoa powder
1 teaspoon bicarbonate of soda

1 Grease and line an 18cm (7 inch) deep, round cake tin (page 8). Preheat the oven to 160°C (325°F/Gas 3).

2 In a large saucepan, warm together the margarine, treacle, syrup and sugar. Add the milk and allow to cool.

3 Beat the eggs, and blend with the cooled mixture. Sift the dry ingredients together into a bowl, add the cooled mixture, and fold in gently with a spatula or tablespoon.

4 Turn the mixture into the prepared tin, and bake in the oven for 1 ¼–1 ¾ hours or until the cake is risen and springy to the touch.

Swiss Roll

MAKES ONE 20CM (8 INCH) SWISS
(JELLY) ROLL
3 eggs
75g (3oz/ ⅓ cup) caster sugar
75g (3oz/ ⅔ cup) plain flour
TO FINISH
Caster sugar
Warmed raspberry jam

1 Grease and line the base of a 30x20cm (12x8 inch) Swiss roll tin (page 8). Preheat the oven to 200°C (400°F/Gas 6).

2 Beat the eggs and caster sugar together in the bowl of an electric mixer, and warm over a pan of hot water. When the mixture is warm, transfer the bowl to the mixer, and whisk at top speed until the mixture has doubled in volume, is light and holds its shape.

3 Sift the flour twice, once on to a sheet of greaseproof paper, and the second time over the mixture. Gently fold in by hand, using open fingertips. Do not overmix.

4 Turn the mixture into the prepared Swiss roll tin, and spread with

a palette knife or spatula to achieve a flat surface. Bake immediately in the oven for approximately 5 minutes only or until the surface of the cake is golden and firm when pressed with fingertips.

5 Immediately turn the Swiss roll over on to a clean tea-towel or sheet of absorbent paper that has been lightly dusted with caster sugar. Remove the lining paper and trim the edges of the cake. Spread warmed raspberry jam over the Swiss roll while it is still hot.

6 Score across the width of the roll approximately 1cm (½ inch) in from a short edge. Roll from the scored edge, using the cloth or

paper as a lever, pulling in a downwards direction to create a tight roll. Leave to cool, then sprinkle with caster sugar.

Genoese Sponge

'Genoese' is a term used to describe a sponge cake with moist eating properties, a firm texture and an even crumb structure. It bakes with a flat top and rises evenly.

MAKES ONE 25x18CM (10x7 INCH) CAKE
100g (4oz/½ cup) margarine
*160g (5½ oz/ 1¼ cups) self-raising sponge
flour*
185g (6 ½ oz/¾ cup) caster sugar
Pinch of salt
2 eggs, beaten
100ml (4fl oz/½ cup) milk
1 tablespoon glycerine
A few drops of vanilla essence

1 Grease and line a 25x18cm (10x7 inch) deep cake tin (page 8). Preheat the oven to 180°C (350°F/Gas 4).

2 Put the margarine in the bowl of an electric mixer with the flour, caster sugar and salt, and crumble together with your fingertips.

3 In a separate bowl, mix the eggs, milk, glycerine and vanilla essence together. Switch the electric mixer on at slow speed, and gradually add

the liquid to the crumbly mixture over 1 minute. Add food colouring if using. Scrape down the mixture before beating for 1 minute on medium speed.

4 Transfer the mixture to the prepared tin and smooth flat with a palette knife. Bake in the oven for approximately 20 minutes or until golden and firm when lightly pressed with your fingertips. The cake should spring back and the fingermarks disappear.

5 Turn the cake out on to a wire rack, peel off the lining paper, and leave to cool.

CUTTING AND PREPARING GENOESE

1 Remove the surface skin of the Genoese with a long, sharp knife. The skin should lift easily away from the body of the cake but be careful not to cut too much cake away. Keeping the knife as flat as possible will help with this. Trim the edges of the cake to remove any crusty or misshapen pieces.

2 Slice horizontally through the cake, using the long, sharp knife and holding it as flat as possible. To keep the cut even, slice through from one side until the knife disappears, turn the cake and repeat with the next side, then turn again and

repeat until all four sides are cut. Continue cutting towards the middle of the cake, turning continuously.

3 Separate the two cut halves of the cake by sliding the top half off. Spread one half with jam or cream and then carefully lift the top half back on, using the flat of your hand to support the cake.

Rich Fruit Cake

The ingredients for this recipe include nougat paste, a smooth paste made commercially from hazelnuts, chocolate and sugar. It is available from cake decorating and sugarcraft shops. Chocolate hazelnut spread can be used as a substitute. For alternative sizes of this cake, see chart on page 138. Cakes made by metric measures will be slightly shallower than those made with imperial measures.

MAKES ONE 20CM (8 INCH) SQUARE CAKE
275g (10oz/ 1¼ cups) butter
275g (10oz/ 1¾ cups) dark soft brown sugar
3 teaspoons glycerine

For alternative sizes of this cake, see chart on page 138.

EXPERT ADVICE

If you are using Genoese cake for building unusual shapes, we don't recommend filling the layers with both jam and cream as the layers will slide apart too easily.

5 teaspoons black treacle
3 teaspoons nougat paste, optional
5 eggs, beaten
275g (10oz/ 2½ cups) plain flour
3 teaspoons ground mixed spice
40g (1½oz/ ½ cup) ground almonds
250g (9oz/ 1½ cups) raisins
250g (9oz/ 1½ cups) currants
500g (1lb 4oz/ 3 cups) sultanas
225g (8oz/ 1⅓ cups) glacé cherries, halved
Grated zest and juice of 1 orange and 1 lemon
4 tablespoons rum or brandy, for maturing

1 Grease and line a 20cm (8 inch) square cake tin (page 8). Preheat the oven to 160°C (325°F/Gas 3), placing a small tin of water on the floor of the oven to create humidity.

2 Put the butter, sugar, glycerine, treacle and nougat paste, if using, in a bowl and cream together until light and fluffy. Add the eggs in four stages, mixing well after each addition. Add the flour, spice and ground almonds, and half mix into the mixture. Add all the fruit, zest and juice of the orange and lemon, and mix well.

3 Turn the mixture into the prepared tin, and bake in the oven for about 3½ hours. Test the cake by inserting a fine skewer into the middle; when removed, the skewer should be clean, with no uncooked mixture attached to it.

4 Remove the cake from the oven and, while still hot, pour over the rum or brandy, assisting its absorption by pricking the surface of the cake with the skewer. Leave the cake to cool.

5 When cold, remove the cake from the tin and peel off the lining paper. Wrap the cake in waxed paper, then foil, and leave to mature, preferably for one month.

Light Fruit Cake

This lighter fruit cake does not need to be left to mature.

MAKES ONE 20CM (8 INCH) SQUARE CAKE

185g (6 ½ oz/ ¾ cup) butter, softened
175g (6oz/ ¼ cup) light golden sugar
4 eggs, beaten
250g (9oz/ 2 ¼ cups) plain flour
1 teaspoon baking powder
Pinch of salt
100g (4oz/ 1 cup) ground almonds
450g (1lb/ 3 cups) mixed fruit, including glacé cherries, glacé pineapple, sultanas, stem ginger and rum-soaked dried apricots, all chopped to the size of the sultanas
Grated zest and juice of 1 orange
A few drops of vanilla essence
2 teaspoons glycerine

1 Grease and line a 20cm (8 inch) square cake tin (page 8). Preheat the oven to 180°C (350°F/Gas 4).

2 Cream the butter and sugar together in a bowl until light and fluffy. Add the eggs in four stages, beating well after each addition. Add the flour, baking powder, salt and ground almonds, and half mix. Add the cleaned fruit, flavourings and glycerine, and mix well.

3 Turn the mixture into the prepared tin, and bake in the oven for 1–1 ½ hours. Test the cake by inserting a skewer in the middle; when the cake is cooked, the skewer should come out clean, with no uncooked mixture attached to it.

4 Leave the cake to cool in the tin, then turn out and peel off the lining paper.

VARIATIONS

NUT TOPPING With such a variety of whole shelled nuts (brazils, walnuts, hazelnuts, pecans, almonds) available in the shops, you can make an attractive topping for a fruit cake by arranging them in patterns on top of the cake. Coat the

top of the cake with warm apricot glaze (page 13), arrange the nuts as required, and leave to set. When set, brush the top of the nuts with warm apricot glaze and leave to set again. Finish by securing a broad, attractive ribbon around the cake.

CRYSTALLIZED FRUIT TOPPING A more colourful (but more expensive) alternative to nuts is to make patterns with crystallized fruit. (The fruit is available in large supermarkets and healthfood shops, but the best selection, used on the cake illustrated, is from Harrods.) Make sure you use crystallized, not dried, fruit: cherries (green, yellow and red), pears, pineapples, oranges, mandarins, kumquats, kiwis, figs, strawberries and angelica are just a few of the fruits available. Some fruit can be purchased whole and, if large, may need to be sliced before use, keeping the smaller fruit whole to create an attractive arrangement. Spread a layer of warm apricot glaze on the cake, then arrange the fruit on top. If desired, glaze the top of the fruit.

MARZIPAN

Marzipan (almond paste) is used for both coating and decorative purposes. It forms a smooth and flawless coating on a cake – the perfect base for royal icing or sugarpaste (rolled fondant), and forms a barrier to prevent moisture from the cake seeping into the sugar coating. As a modelling medium, marzipan is easy to handle and pliable, and can be coloured by kneading in food colouring. The illustration above shows a round of homemade marzipan, which is easy to make if you prefer not to use commercial brands.

Homemade Marzipan

Homemade marzipan has a grainier texture than commercially made marzipan, which is passed through heavy rollers to create the totally smooth texture with which we are familiar. The flavour of homemade marzipan can be adjusted to taste by adding more or less almond essence, and the colour of the almonds can be maintained by mixing in a glass or glazed bowl (a metal bowl can give the marzipan a greyish tinge). When using raw egg, there is always a risk of salmonella, so use homemade marzipan quickly, and ensure that you wash your hands well between separating the egg and mixing the marzipan.

225g (8oz/1½ cups) icing (confectioners') sugar
225g (8oz/2 cups) ground almonds
1 large egg white
1 teaspoon lemon juice
A few drops of almond essence

1 Place the icing sugar and ground almonds in a bowl, add the liquid ingredients and stir together. Knead the mixture until smooth.

2 Store in a polythene bag until ready to use. Use within a week of making.

APRICOT GLAZE

This can be made in any quantity and is brushed on a cake before coating with marzipan. Sieve some apricot jam into a saucepan and bring to the boil. Add water, 1 tablespoon at a time, until the glaze will coat the back of a metal spoon in a thin layer. Bring to the boil again, and use as required. Apricot glaze can be stored in the refrigerator in a clean jar with a tightly fitting lid. After storing, bring to the boil again, and use while hot.

COATING WITH MARZIPAN

To obtain a flat surface to your cake, turn the cake upside-down. If the cake has peaked during baking or has an uneven surface, trim it level before turning the cake over. To avoid wasting too much cake, you might be able to turn the cake upside-down without too much trimming, if any; gaps at the bottom edge can be packed with small pieces of marzipan before the whole surface is coated.

ALL-IN-ONE METHOD

This method of coating a cake with marzipan creates a good base for sugarpaste, and is suitable for all shapes of cake.

1 Turn the cake upside-down. Measure the cake across the top and down two opposite sides. Add

2.5cm (1 inch) to this measurement. Brush the top and sides of the cake with boiled apricot glaze.

2 Knead the marzipan into a smooth ball and roll it out on a work surface or non-stick board dusted with icing (confectioners') sugar, turning the marzipan occasionally to prevent sticking and to keep it circular, until the required diameter is reached. The thickness of the marzipan can vary depending upon personal choice. Lift the marzipan away from the work surface, using the rolling pin as a support, and lower it over the surface of the cake, placing the marzipan against the side of the cake first.

3 Smooth the marzipan down with your hands, firstly across the top of the cake with the flat of your

---

EXPERT ADVICE

If a fold appears in the marzipan, lift the marzipan outwards, and then gently ease it in again, smoothing gradually downwards. Do not attempt to press the fold in as this will result in an uneven surface.

hand, then over the edges with your hands slightly cupped. Smooth the sides of the cake, again with the flat of your hand, and with a slight upwards movement.

4 Smooth the marzipan down to the bottom of the cake, and trim off any excess with a sharp knife. Give the cake a final polish with the flat of your hands and leave to dry or crust for a few hours.

TOP AND SIDES METHOD

For this method of coating a cake with marzipan, the top and sides are coated separately, creating strong (90°) edges suitable for coating with royal icing.

1 Turn the cake upside-down and pack the bottom edges with marzipan to obtain a smooth finish, if necessary. Brush the top surface with boiled apricot glaze. Roll out the marzipan on a work surface or non-stick board dusted with icing

---

(confectioners') sugar until the marzipan is slightly larger than the cake top and the thickness required. Lower the jammed surface of the cake on to the marzipan and trim with a sharp knife. Turn the cake back over.

2 For a round cake, brush the sides with apricot glaze. Roll out the marzipan into a long strip and trim to the length of the circumference of the cake. Trim to the depth of the cake plus 1cm (½ inch), dust with a little icing sugar to stop the marzipan sticking, and roll it up. Unroll the marzipan around the side of the cake, trim to fit, and trim the top edge with a sharp knife.

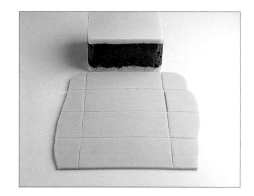

3 For a cake with corners, brush alternate sides with apricot glaze. Roll out the marzipan into a rectangle slightly wider than the length of one side of the cake, and long enough to coat all the sides (i.e. four times the depth of one side for a square cake, and six times for a

hexagon, and so on). Cut out the required number of side pieces, making each one slightly taller than the cake and slightly wider than the width of the cake.

4 Position the first side of marzipan and smooth into place. Trim the top, cutting inwards towards the centre of the cake. This makes a good seal. Trim the marzipan to fit at the corners. Turn the cake and repeat, brushing with glaze when necessary.

Battenburg Cake

This traditional cake is usually made from pieces of pink and white Genoese sponge, glued together with jam. The whole is then coated in a thin layer of marzipan.

Pink Genoese sponge (page 10)
Plain Genoese sponge
2 tablespoons raspberry or strawberry jam
225g (8oz) pink marzipan (almond paste)
Icing (confectioners') sugar
Apricot glaze (page 13)

1 Trim the two pieces of Genoese to the same size – about 20cm (8 inches) long, 5cm (2 inches) wide

and 2.5cm (1 inch) deep. Spread the top of one piece with raspberry or strawberry jam, and place the other piece on top.

2 Cut through the two layers lengthwise to produce two long strips, each with a square of pink and a square of white when viewed from the end. (Use a cutting guide if you have one.) Turn both pieces of cake on to their sides and spread one with jam. Lift the other piece on to the jam to produce a checker-board effect at the end.

3 Roll out the marzipan on a work surface dusted with icing sugar, into a rectangle of the required thickness, and trim to the size of the cake. The marzipan rectangle should be as wide as the length of the cake, and long enough to cover all four sides of the Battenburg. Spread a thin layer of boiled apricot glaze over the surface of the marzipan. Lift the cake on to the marzipan, aligning the edge of the cake with the edge of the marzipan. Roll the cake along the marzipan until the four sides are coated, with the join underneath. Trim away any surplus marzipan.

4 While the marzipan is still soft, crimp the top edges of the cake. Hand crimping is a traditional finish for a Battenburg; pinch the marzipan edge between your thumb and forefinger (or your thumb and the knuckle of your forefinger). Finally, trim the two edges for a neat finish.

5 To complete the decoration, colour some marzipan as desired, cut out shapes with a small blossom cutter, and attach to the top of the cake with a little boiled water. Serve in slices.

Marzipan Modelling

Marzipan (almond paste) is a good modelling medium as it remains soft and pliable for some time, and can be coloured easily. Although you can make a special paste for modelling with 'raw' marzipan (a commercially made paste which has a high almond content), the readily available bought marzipans can all be used.

Keep the marzipan in polythene bags when you are not using it. Try not to overknead the paste as it can become oily as the almond oil is worked out. If this happens, mix in a few drops of orange flower or rose water, leave to rest in a polythene bag and wash your hands in cool water. If the marzipan is sticky, wipe your fingers with a damp cloth. It is a good idea to keep a damp cloth beside you at all times when modelling with marzipan. Generally, freshly modelled pieces will stick to themselves, but if they have dried, glue them together with a little melted white chocolate. Don't use royal icing as this will crack away from the marzipan as it dries.

Basic Shapes

All modelling starts with a ball. As well as being a shape in itself, the process of rolling a ball will ensure a perfectly smooth surface from which to model everything else.

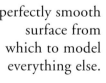

1 To make a ball, knead the paste lightly, place it in the palms of your hands and rotate. Keep your fingers well stretched out to polish the marzipan smooth as it rolls around.

2 For a pear shape, roll a ball, then open the palms of your hands and rock them backwards and forwards. Pressure from the sides of your hands will thin one side, while the thicker side protrudes between your thumbs.

3 For a sausage shape, again start by rolling a ball. Although a sausage can be modelled in your hands, for a bump-free, perfectly smooth finish, use an icing polisher and roll the paste backwards and forwards on a hard surface or non-stick board.

Marzipan Animals

Basic marzipan animals are usually modelled to the same general size, whether making a chick or an elephant, although we can appreciate that in real life, a chick and an elephant are at the opposite ends of the scale! 'Cute' features are common on marzipan animals – big eyes and cheeky expressions.

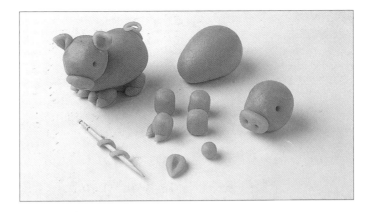

CHICK

Colour approximately 25g (1oz) marzipan as required, and separate off about one third to make two wings from flattened pear shapes. Roll the remaining piece into two balls, one larger than the other, and use the larger ball for the chick's body and the smaller ball for its head. Shape a beak and comb, and mark the wings with a knife. Add eyes made from tiny flattened balls of paste.

PIG

Colour approximately 25g (1oz) marzipan as required, and separate off about one third. Roll the larger piece into a shape for the body, and use the remainder to shape the head and feet. Twist a fine sausage of paste around a cocktail stick (toothpick) to shape a tail. Add ears, a snout and trotters, and mark eyes and nostrils with a cocktail stick.

DUCK

Colour approximately 25g (1oz) marzipan as required, and separate off about one third. Roll the larger piece into a pear shape for the body, lifting the pointed end slightly to form the duck's tail. Roll the remaining marzipan into a ball for the head, and shape wings and a beak. Use a piping tube (tip) to mark the wings.

ELEPHANT

Colour approximately 40g (1 ½ oz) marzipan as required, and shape two thirds into a sausage for the body. Cut and open each end of the sausage to make legs, and cut a tail in the paste with scissors. Shape the head from the remaining one third, firstly by making a pear shape, then by rolling the trunk from the thinner end of the pear. Add ears, eyes, and trunk markings, as shown.

The little leprechaun is an example of the next step in marzipan modelling, from modelled coloured shapes to assembling more detailed pieces and mixing colours.

Marzipan Tea Fancies

Marzipan is a wonderful medium for texturing and colouring, producing many different effects, as illustrated by these dainty tea fancies. To make them, cut Genoese sponge into a variety of shapes, generally no larger than 3.5cm (1½ inches) overall. Brush the shapes with boiled apricot glaze, then coat with a *thin* layer of marzipan textured to the finish required. Decorate with shaped pieces or cutouts.

Marzipan Fruits

All the fruits illustrated are modelled from the basic ball, pear and sausage shapes described on page 16. Colour the marzipan as required and add texture to appropriate fruits by indenting all over with the end of a paintbrush (strawberry), or rolling on a nutmeg grater (orange and lemon). Add stalks, calyxes and leaves as required: for the strawberry, the calyx is cut from thinly rolled green marzipan using a small calyx cutter; the orange stalk and the base of the apple are cloves with their seed pods removed; the apple and pear stalks are very thinly rolled sausages of brown marzipan.

Add extra colour to the fruits by dusting with petal dusts (blossom tints) in appropriate colours, using a soft brush. Alternatively, use a fine paintbrush or a sponge and liquid colours.

Small marzipan fruits make delicious petits fours. Life–sized versions can be arranged attractively in a bowl and used as a table decoration or centrepiece.

SUGARPASTE

Sometimes called rolled fondant or ready-to-roll icing, sugarpaste has now become very popular amongst both professional and amateur cake-decorators. It can be used to coat any type of cake and is easy to apply, providing a smooth, clean finish that is firm when set, yet soft to cut and eat. It can also be used in a number of decorative ways: when freshly applied and still soft, it is the ideal medium for texturing techniques such as crimping and embossing, and many of the cake-decorating skills adapted from needlework and other crafts, such as quilting and stencilling, can be worked in sugarpaste to great effect; once firm, sugarpaste provides a good base for piping and other finishing touches. Strengthened with gum tragacanth, the paste can also be used for modelling decorative shapes, and sets firm enough to be used for free-standing figures.

COATING WITH SUGARPASTE

Sugarpaste can be used to coat any cake, but for a fruit cake we recommend applying a layer of marzipan (almond paste) first (page 13). For sponge cakes, the sugarpaste can be applied directly to the cake, with just a thin masking of apricot glaze (page13) or buttercream.

Whatever type and shape of cake you are covering, the first step is to colour the sugarpaste (if necessary), and then to roll it out. Sugarpaste is available in many colours as well as in white, and you can create the exact colour required by kneading in liquid or paste food colourings. Colouring techniques such as marbling and stencilling (pages 25 and 46) can greatly enhance the appearance of the finished cake.

Sugarpaste should preferably be rolled out with a non-stick rolling pin on a non-stick board, using a little icing (confectioners') sugar to prevent sticking. You should use the least amount of icing sugar possible, especially when rolling paste for the top surface of the cake. *Never use cornflour* for rolling out sugarpaste for coating as cornflour is uncooked starch which, when mixed with moisture and sugar, can cause the marzipan to ferment, and the sugarpaste to lift and crack.

COATING THE CAKE

1 For a fruit cake, brush the surface of the marzipan with cool boiled water or clear alcohol (gin or vodka). If coating a sponge cake, brush the surface with boiled apricot glaze or spread with a thin layer of buttercream. Knead the required amount of sugarpaste with your hands to soften and give a smooth surface.

2 Measure the cake across the top and down both sides, and roll out the paste to fit, allowing an extra 2.5cm (1 inch) for trimming. The thicker the paste, the easier it will be to coat the cake, but bear in mind that a thick layer can be too sweet and overpower the flavours and textures of the cake and marzipan. We recommend rolling out the sugarpaste to a thickness of 5mm (¼ inch). Ensure that the paste does not stick to the board by turning the paste regularly as you roll it. Polish the surface of the sugarpaste with the flat of your hand to remove any excess icing sugar and to check that there are no air bubbles in the paste.

3 Lift the paste over the rolling pin, and use the rolling pin to position the paste on the side of the cake, over the top and down the other side.

4 Smooth the top of the cake with the flat of your hand, starting from the centre and working outwards. This will ensure that you have not trapped any air between the sugarpaste and the surface beneath. If you do find an air bubble, either lift the paste up quickly with one hand and smooth down again with the other or, if the sugarpaste is now firmly stuck down, prick the bubble with a pin and smooth the hole with your fingertips.

5 Work your way from the top of the cake down the sides, smoothing evenly. As folds in the sugarpaste appear, lift the bottom edge out to

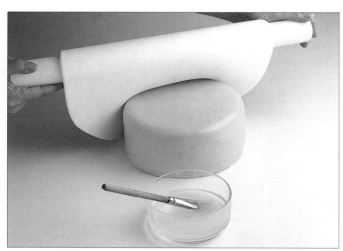

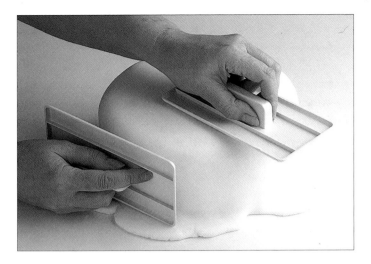

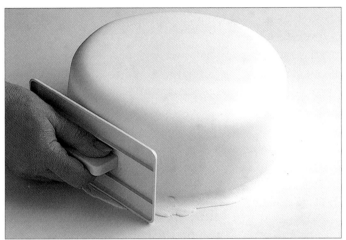

remove the fold and then gently press the paste back on to the surface of the cake. Continue smoothing downwards, using icing polishers if desired.

6 Using a sharp knife, trim away the excess paste from around the bottom of the cake, leaving an overlap of 1cm (½ inch).

7 Smooth over the whole cake again with the flat of your hands or icing polishers, flattening the paste at the bottom of the cake to produce perpendicular sides.

8 Trim all round the bottom edge of the paste again to attain a clean, neat finish.

COATING THE BOARD

All cake boards and drums are finished with silver, gold or coloured metallic paper to provide a strong and hygienic surface on which to place your cake. Although the boards can be attractive and are sometimes incorporated in the overall design of the cake, it is common practice these days to coat the board as well as the cake with icing, giving the cake a more 'complete' appearance. You should ensure that the base of your cake is in contact with the hygienic surface of the board; decorative finishes, whether in sugar, paper or material, should only be applied to the area of the board around the cake base. Alternatively, place the cake on a

thin board the same size as the cake before placing it on the coated drum or board.

When cake and board are both covered, leave the sugarpaste to dry before decorating.

EXPERT ADVICE

When coating a cake with corners, roll out and apply the paste in the same way as for a round cake. Smooth the top first (step 4), then before smoothing the sides, make sure the sugarpaste is neatly fitted on to the corners. Smooth the sides in the same way as for a round cake, i.e. lift out and press in (step 5).

CAKE AND BOARD TOGETHER

1 Place the cake on the board. Roll out the sugarpaste, allowing extra for the board. Lift the paste as if coating the cake, this time positioning the paste on the edge of the board first, then the side, top and opposite side of the cake, and finally, the far side of the board.

2 Smooth from the centre of the top of the cake, down the sides and finally over the board. Trim excess paste away from the edge of the board with a sharp knife.

COATING WITH A STRIP OF PASTE

1 Coat the cake in sugarpaste as described on page 20, and place on a cake board (taking care not to mark the soft sugarpaste). Roll a

EXPERT ADVICE

Cake drums are 1cm (½ inch) thick and are used for heavy fruit and other cakes where a firm supporting base is required. Cake boards (sometimes called double thick boards) are used for light fruit and sponge cakes.

sausage of sugarpaste with your hands, and then roll it into a strip with a rolling pin.

2 Use a tape measure or length of string to judge the length required. Trim the two long sides of the strip to the width required plus approximately 1cm (½ inch). Quickly roll up the strip, moisten the board with cool boiled water, and then unroll the paste directly on to the board.

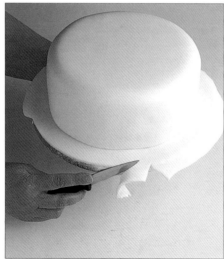

3 Cut the join to fit, and smooth the paste down with the pads of your fingers, particularly over the join. Trim as required around the board edge with a sharp knife. Finish by polishing the cut edge of the paste with the tips of your fingers.

COATING THE BOARD AND REMOVING THE CENTRE

1 Coat the cake in sugarpaste as described on page 20, and allow to set firm overnight. Cut a paper tem-

plate the size and shape of the coated cake. Brush *the edge only* of a cake board with cool boiled water. Roll out the sugarpaste and coat the surface of the board. Place the template where the cake will sit and cut around the edge with a sharp knife. Remove the template and the sugarpaste beneath it.

2 Lift the cake and lower it gently into the hole in the sugarpaste. Smooth the soft paste on the board into the join between it and the cake

Girl and Boy Cake

MATERIALS
1kg (2½ lb) sugarpaste
Selection of food colourings
25cm (10 inch) square cake drum
Genoese sponge (page 10)
Apricot glaze (page 13) or buttercream (page 115)
Small amount of flower paste (page 84)

EQUIPMENT
Icing polishers
Dresden tool
Claygun, optional
Plunger blossom cutter

1 Colour 225g (8oz) sugarpaste green and use to coat the cake drum, including the edges.

2 Make paper templates of the girl and boy (page 131), and place on the Genoese. Cut around the outlines with a sharp knife. Carve away the Genoese not required, following the templates and the photographs (above). Mask the cake with apricot glaze or buttercream.

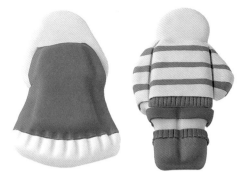

3 Coat both shapes in a thin layer of flesh-coloured sugarpaste, pressing the paste into the carved layers with your fingertips.

4 For the girl, make a petticoat in white sugarpaste, place on the cake, and cut to fit. Use a dresden tool to mark in the grooves. Use blue sugarpaste to make the dress, and fit into position, trimming as required. For the boy, cut and fit green socks with blue tops, and texture with the dresden tool. Add blue shorts and a green and white striped shirt made using inlay techniques (page 26). Texture the bottom welt of the shirt with the dresden tool.

5 Next, for the girl, add an apron, collar, arms and shoes. Add the boy's collar and arrange his left arm to hold a brown paste ball.

6 To make the girl's hair, roll some long, thin strands of a half-and-half mixture of sugarpaste and flower paste. (Use a claygun if you have one.) Plait the strands into pigtails and position on the girl's head. Paint facial features on both figures; finish the girl by adding flowers, and the boy by adding his hair and boots.

7 Lift the girl and boy into position on the coated drum.

DECORATING WITH SUGARPASTE

Sugarpaste can be used in a huge variety of ways to add decorative touches to a cake, ranging from simple embossing and crimping to more advanced inlay work, broderie anglaise and stencilling. Many of the techniques in this chapter are derived from other crafts, such as needlework and leatherwork, but all adapt beautifully to sugarpaste.

SCRIBING

This technique is carried out when the sugarpaste coating on a cake is still soft. It makes use of the effect of shadows in grooves marked in the sugarpaste with a veining tool. Plan your pattern on paper first because if you make a mistake you will have to recoat the cake.

STRAIGHT-LINE SCRIBING Use an icing ruler and a veining tool to draw a variety of straight lines across the surface of the cake. This technique is used to great effect on the Sunburst Cake (right).

FREEHAND SCRIBING Curved lines can be scribed freehand on to the cake's surface. The lines can be continued from the board, up the side

of the cake, across the top, and down the other side to create one overall design.

Sunburst Cake

MATERIALS
20cm (8 inch) square cake
Apricot glaze (page 13)
1kg (2lb) marzipan (almond paste)
25cm (10 inch) square cake drum
1kg (2lb) sugarpaste, coloured with melon paste food colouring
Selection of food colourings
Clear alcohol (gin or vodka)

EQUIPMENT
Icing polishers
Veining tool
Icing ruler
5cm (2 inch) round cutter
Piece of sponge

1 Brush the cake with apricot glaze and coat with marzipan (page 13). Leave to set for a few hours. Place on the cake drum.

2 Coat the cake and cake drum (including the edges) in sugarpaste (page 22).

3 Using a veining tool and icing ruler, draw a line in the sugarpaste 2.5cm (1 inch) up

from the base of the cake. Draw another line 2.5cm (1 inch) above the first. This produces the 'ribbon' border.

4 Again using the ruler and veining tool, draw a square on the top of the cake, positioning it towards one corner. Draw another square 1cm (½ inch) outside the first.

5 Scribe lines from the bottom of the side border, down the sides of the cake, across the board and then down the edges of the board.

6 Scribe in sunray lines from one corner of the square pattern, using the ruler to keep them straight.

7 Cut a circle of yellow sugarpaste, approximately 5cm (2 inches) in diameter, and cut into quarters. Attach one quarter in the corner of the square on the top of the cake.

8 To complete, colour the borders on the top and sides of the cake, using the sponging technique (page 25), masking uncoloured areas with pieces of greaseproof paper.

SPONGING

Sponging is a useful technique to use when you need to make colour changes on a cake after the base colour has been applied. Fading effects are also possible, and sponging with masks, templates and stencils gives a wide range of finishes.

1 Mix liquid, paste or powder food colouring (petal dust/blossom tint) with alcohol (gin or vodka) to the required colour. Tear a small piece of sponge from a larger block, dip it into the colour and squeeze the sponge. Test the effect by dabbing the sponge over a spare piece of sugarpaste before applying to the finished surface.

2 Mask off any areas you don't want coloured with a paper template. Sponge until the area is covered as required.

3 Remove the mask to reveal the unsponged area, taking care not to smudge the colour. Leave to dry.

TEXTURING IN SHEETS

Fine texturing can be achieved over large areas of cake by using perspex sheeting. Ensure that the perspex sheet is clean and polished dry with a clean tea-towel. Roll the sugarpaste out on a non-stick board to the thickness required. Lift the sugarpaste with the aid of the rolling pin on to the perspex sheet, and roll once only, using medium pressure. Cut out the required shapes of textured sugarpaste and lift them away from the perspex.

MARBLING

Sugarpaste is so easy to colour that many exciting effects can be achieved by blending and half-blending colours into the paste, creating a 'marbled' appearance.

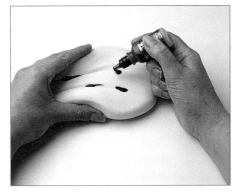

1 Knead the required amount of sugarpaste well and drop on liquid or paste colouring. Fold the sugarpaste, twisting occasionally, until the colour starts to spread through the paste in streaks.

2 Roll out the sugarpaste on a non-stick surface. Roll particularly firmly in the direction in which you wish the streaks to run.

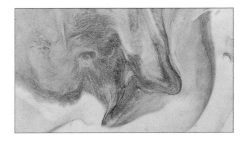

3 Further effects can be achieved by using a coloured or marbled piece of sugarpaste, and then applying strips of differently coloured sugarpaste to it.

4 Work the strips into the main piece of sugarpaste with your fingers and thumbs, pressing the coloured paste into a marbled effect. Roll out and polish as required.

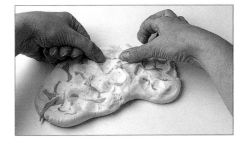

INLAY WORK

Patterns can be created over the whole surface of a cake by inlaying pieces of sugarpaste into the base coating. This technique is also useful for smaller patterned shapes which can be cut out and applied to the cake.

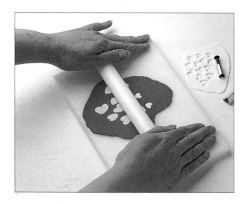

1 Colour the background sugarpaste and roll out to the required size. Cover with a sheet of clingfilm (plastic wrap) to stop the sugarpaste drying out. Cut the patterning pieces out of another piece of sugarpaste in a contrasting colour, and arrange these on the background sugarpaste (from which you have removed the clingfilm). Roll the paste once in one direction.

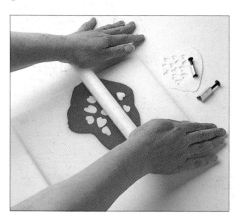

2 Roll the paste again, in the opposite direction, to even up the patterned pieces. Apply immediately to the cake or prepared surface.

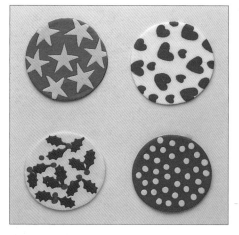

3 The inlay technique can be used to create many different patterns and effects.

Clown Cake

MATERIALS
20cm (8 inch) round cake
Apricot glaze (page 13)
1kg (2lb) marzipan (almond paste)
Icing (confectioners') sugar
1kg (2lb) sugarpaste
Selection of food colourings
25cm (10 inch) round cake drum
Clear alcohol (gin or vodka)
Ribbon to trim cake drum

EQUIPMENT
Set of plain round cutters
Icing polishers
Clown cutter (Cake Art)
Set of scalloped round cutters
No. 0 paintbrush

1 Brush the cake with apricot glaze, and coat with marzipan using the top and sides method on page 14 to obtain a 90° angle at the top edge.

2 Roll out some white sugarpaste. Brush the top of the cake only with cool boiled water, and coat with sugarpaste, trimming around the edge carefully with a knife.

3 Roll out a sheet of sugarpaste, slightly longer than the circumference and slightly wider than the depth of the cake. Following the techniques for inlay work (left), create the spotted pattern. Brush the sides of the cake with cool boiled water and apply the spotted paste, fitting the bottom in neatly, trimming the join and finally trimming the top edge. Polish well and leave to dry before placing the cake on the cake drum and coating the board using the strip method (page 22).

4 The clown is made using a commercial cutter. The base shape is cut out as one piece of white sugarpaste and the various parts of the clothing and body added afterwards, colouring small pieces of sugarpaste as you need them. To create stripes or checks for the clown's trousers, roll out the base colour sugarpaste, then roll out some sugarpaste thinly in a contrasting colour and cut into strips or small squares. Moisten very slightly and place on the base colour sugarpaste, arranging in stripes or a chequered design. Roll over in both directions, then cut as required.

5 The hair is made by pushing coloured sugarpaste through a sieve. The facial features are painted on with a fine paintbrush (no. 0 or smaller), using liquid colours or paste colours mixed with alcohol.

6 A twisted rope of sugarpaste (page 35) is applied to the bottom edge of the cake, glued in position with a little cool boiled water. To make the top 'circus ring', roll a long sausage of sugarpaste and form it into a ring. Smooth the join. Moisten the top edge of the cake and position the ring.

CRIMPING

One of the oldest decorating techniques, originally called 'pinching' and used on marzipan, has now been updated and modernized with many new jaw designs and a transfer from brass to stainless steel tools.

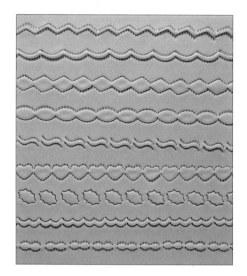

CRIMPED PATTERNS Here is a selection of patterns created with different crimpers. Note how the shapes cast shadows.

TOP-EDGE CRIMPING Crimping around the top edge of a cake as soon as the sugarpaste coating has been applied gives a quick, easy finish which resembles a piped royal icing finish (which would be much more time-consuming).

CRIMPED ROPES Rope effects can be achieved by crimping sausages of sugarpaste positioned around the base of the cake.

BOTTOM-EDGE CRIMPING A quick way of sealing the cake to the cake drum or board is to crimp the bottom edge. An attractive pattern is achieved at the same time.

CRIMPING LARGE AREAS Crimping is generally used in lines, and yet beautiful padded and textured effects can be achieved by building up patterns of crimping. With about 20 different crimpers available, many interesting alternatives are possible. Set the jaws of the crimper at the correct width (often a rubber band is supplied to help with this) and push into the sugarpaste. Squeeze gently, release the pressure and remove the crimper. To stop the crimper sticking to the sugarpaste, either dip the jaws into cornflour or wipe regularly with a barely damp, clean cloth. Alternatively, smear the jaws with a little white vegetable fat (shortening).

SMOCKING

This very attractive technique is adapted from needlecraft. The effect can be achieved with or without the use of piped royal icing.

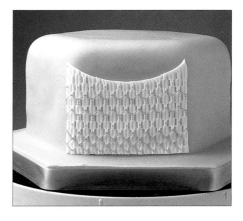

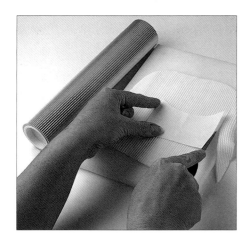

1 Make a template of the area you wish to cover. Roll out sugarpaste to 2.5mm (⅛ inch) thick with a plain rolling pin, and roll again using a smocking or ribbed rolling pin. Use medium pressure to obtain deep ribs and to thin the paste to approximately 1.75mm (¹⁄₁₆ inch). Place the template on the paste and cut around the edge with a sharp knife.

2 Moisten the back of the smocked paste with a little cool boiled water, and place in position on the cake.

3 Using ordinary tweezers or smocking tweezers, pinch in the pattern while the sugarpaste is still soft. Leave to harden.

4 Colour royal icing as required and pipe in the stitch patterns with a no. 1 or no. 2 tube (tip). Leave to dry.

5 Finish the cut edge of the smocked area neatly. Here, a Garrett frill (page 38) and piped royal icing have been used.

QUILTING

This technique, derived from needlecraft, is an effective way of combining crimping and patterning skills.

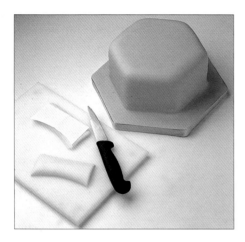

1 Make a template of the area you wish to cover with the quilting. Roll out sugarpaste to approximately 5mm (¼ inch) thick, and cut around the template with a sharp knife. Smooth the edges of the shape and press lightly to create a cushion effect. Trim to the required shape again, and smooth with fingertips to soften the cut edges. Be careful not to distort the shape.

2 Moisten the back of the shape with a little cool boiled water and gently lift into position.

3 Using a large straight crimper, crimp a quilted pattern on to the padded paste. Add dots to the pattern with the end of a paintbrush (see TIM Birthday Cake, opposite).

TIM Birthday Cake

MATERIALS
15cm (6 inch) hexagonal cake, measured point to point
Apricot glaze (page 13)
700g (1½lb) marzipan (almond paste)
20cm (8 inch) round or hexagonal cake drum, measured straight edge to straight edge
Icing (confectioners') sugar
450g (1lb) pale blue sugarpaste
225g (8oz) cream or champagne sugarpaste
Small amount of darker blue flower paste (page 84) for 'ribbon'
Small amount of royal icing made with pure albumen (page 50)
Ribbon (sugar or fabric) to trim cake drum

EQUIPMENT
Icing polishers
Large straight crimper
Icing ruler
Tailor's wheel, optional
Single ribbon insertion tool
Bow cutter, optional
Dresden tool

1 Brush the cake with apricot glaze and coat in marzipan, using the all-in-one method (page 13). Leave to crust overnight.

2 Place the cake on the cake drum, brush the marzipan with cool boiled water, and coat the cake and drum in pale blue sugarpaste (page 22).

3 Quilt the sides of the cake with cream or champagne sugarpaste as shown left. Using the same quilting techniques, cut a disc of sugarpaste 1cm (½ inch) thick, and round the edges with your fingertips. Place in the centre of the top of the cake, securing with cool boiled water, and quilt the edge to match the sides of the cake.

4 Apply the sugar ribbon insertion and bows while the sugarpaste is still workable (pages 32–33).

5 Using templates from page 132, make the runout letters (page 71) for the top of the cake, and leave to dry for 24 hours. Arrange the dried letters on the cake and when you have them in the correct position, fix to the cake with a small amount of soft royal icing.

6 Complete the presentation with a ribbon, either fabric or sugar (flower paste), attached to the edge of the cake drum.

RIBBON INSERTION

This is another fabric technique which has transferred well to sugarpaste. The ribbon used can be either fabric or made from flower paste (page 84). When selecting a fabric ribbon for this technique, choose a firm one. To ensure neat cuts, the coated cake should be left until the surface of the sugarpaste has crusted but it is still soft underneath.

1 Make a paper template of the shape required, and make evenly spaced pencil marks along its edge corresponding to the required length of the ribbon inserts and the gaps in between. Place the template on the cake and hold in position with a small amount of masking tape.

2 Cut the ribbon to the required lengths, ensuring that the cut edges are neat and not frayed. Place the ribbon in a double-edged ribbon insertion tool and hold in place with the tips of your fingers.

3 Gently press the ribbon insertion tool into the sugarpaste, using the marked template as a guide. The tool will cut the sugarpaste and push the ribbon into the cake at the same time. Lift the tool away.

EXPERT ADVICE

If you use fabric ribbon on a cake, ensure that it is all removed before the cake is cut as it is not edible and can cause choking.

SUGAR RIBBON INSERTION

This technique allows you to determine the exact size and colour of the ribbon you wish to use rather than relying on what fabric ribbons you can obtain in the shops. Sugar ribbons should be made from flower paste (page 84).

1 Colour some flower paste as required and roll out thinly. To cre-

ate a silky effect, dust the surface with an edible lustre powder (petal dust/blossom tint), such as silver snowflake.

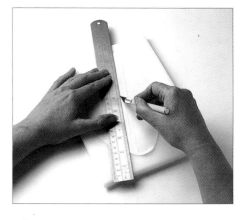

2 Using a metal ruler to guide you, cut the paste into strips with a scalpel. Mark a line of 'stitches' just inside each edge of each strip using a tailor's wheel (optional). Cover the strips of paste with clingfilm (plastic wrap) to prevent them drying out.

3 Make a paper template of the required shape and make evenly

spaced pencil marks along its edges to act as a guide for the ribbon inserts. Hold the template in position and cut slits in the surface of the sugarpaste with a single ribbon insertion tool or a scalpel. Remove the template.

4 Cut the strips of paste to the required lengths and, with the aid of the single ribbon insertion tool, push the paste into the slots.

SUGAR BOWS

These provide a neat finish to ribbon insertion and other techniques. Sugar bows can be cut by hand from strips created as for sugar ribbon insertion (opposite). Alternatively, you can use commercial bow cutters.

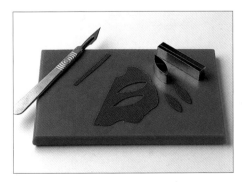

1 Colour some flower paste and roll it out thinly on a non-stick board. Cut out the shapes required with bow cutters, and neaten the cut edges with a scalpel.

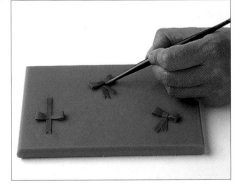

2 Fold the paste to create the two loops of the bow, and position over the straight strip. Fold the strip over the join of the loops and tuck in position with a dresden tool.

3 Sugar bows look most attractive used in combination with sugar ribbon insertion and an embossed edge (page 34).

EMBOSSING

Originating from leatherwork, embossing is very suitable for use on sugarpaste or marzipan. Many different embossers are available commercially and you can make your own embossing tools with carved buttons, jewellery, etc. (very well cleaned).

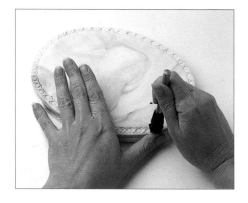

1 Coat the surface area with sugarpaste and immediately start to emboss while the paste is still soft. When working along an edge, use the ball of your thumb to guide the embosser into the correct position.

2 Textured patterns can be created by repeating the embossing technique in small areas. Here a small flower embosser has been used to create a lilac design.

3 Enhance the embossed patterns with colour, if required, using paste, liquid or powder food colourings mixed with clear alcohol and painted on with a fine brush.

4 To complete the embossed design, add lettering in royal icing (page 82).

5 This coated drum shows a crimped edge with embossed patterns. All the patterned areas have been painted with food colours.

EXPERT ADVICE

Liquid food colours are water based, so can be diluted with water, if necessary. Paste or powder colours work better if diluted with alcohol.

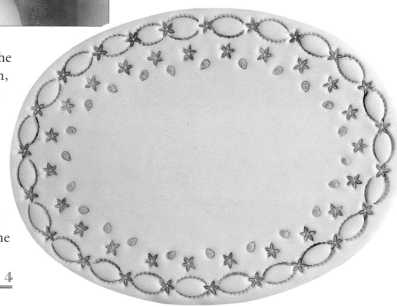

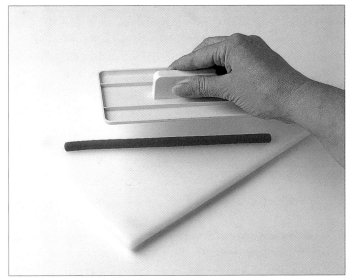

6 This board has been coated in white sugarpaste, then a lilac padded outer edge has been applied and then crimped with a curved crimper. The pattern has been completed with an embosser tool and the finer detail added with piped royal icing.

ROPES AND PLAITS

A simple and colourful finish for many cakes can be achieved by using sugar ropes and plaits, particu-larly on novelty and children's cakes. The most suitable medium is sug-arpaste or marzipan, but fine ropes and plaits can also be made with flower paste.

1 Colour some paste and roll with your hand on a board to create a long, smooth sausage shape.

2 An icing polisher can be used to achieve a very even roll.

3 Using contrasting colours, vary-ing thicknesses of paste, and differ-ent braiding patterns, a variety of rope and plait styles can be created. See the Clown Cake on page 27, and the rag doll's hair on page 44.

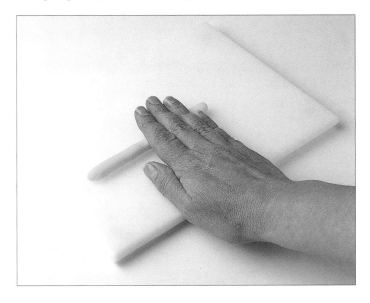

DRAPES AND BOWS

This technique gives a soft effect to cakes; the strengthened sugarpaste easily folds into the required swags.

1 Mix 1 teaspoon gum tragacanth into 225g (8oz) sugarpaste. Measure the part of the cake across which the drape will be positioned and add 2.5cm (1 inch) to this measurement. Measure the width required, approximately 5cm (2 inches), and cut a template this size. Roll out the paste quite thinly and cut out the shape, using the template and a sharp knife or scalpel.

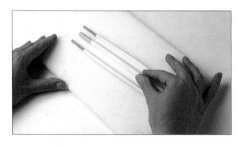

2 Lift the paste on to three dowel rods which are laid parallel 1cm (½ inch) apart. Ease the paste down and around the dowels.

3 Remove the rods, leaving the paste in its curved shape. Pinch the ends of the paste together.

4 Moisten the surface of the cake where the drape will sit with a little cool boiled water. Lift the drape by the pinched ends only and gently shake it to encourage a curve. Place the drape in position on the cake and ensure it is firmly fixed. Trim away any excess paste. Cover the ends of the drapes with sugarpaste bows (see below).

5 To make a bow, roll out some more strengthened paste, and cut out two rectangles that are slightly smaller than those cut for the drapes. Use a dowel rod to shape the ends. Pinch the ends, then fold the paste in half lengthways and glue with cool boiled water. Cut two tails from rectangles of paste and attach in position on the cake. Add the bow loops. Cut a smaller rectangle of paste and lightly pleat for the bow knot. Moisten the position on the bow loops and wrap the knot piece around. Cut away any excess paste and rub the join smooth with a small modelling tool.

Bows and Drapes Cake

MATERIALS
20cm (8 inch) round cake
Apricot glaze (page 13)
900g (2lb) marzipan (almond paste)
25cm (10 inch) round cake drum
800g (1¾lb) sea green sugarpaste
(coloured with ice blue and mint green paste food colourings)
Silver snowflake lustre powder
Clear alcohol (gin or vodka)
400g (14oz) white sugarpaste
1 teaspoon gum tragacanth
2 royal icing doves, optional

EQUIPMENT
Icing polishers
Piece of sponge
Dowel rods
Heart cutters

1 Brush the cake with apricot glaze and coat in marzipan using the all-in-one method (page 13).

2 Place the cake on the cake drum. Moisten the cake with cool boiled water and coat the cake and drum in sea green sugarpaste (page 22). Leave to dry.

3 Mix some sea green colouring (made by mixing ice blue and mint green) with silver snowflake dust and alcohol, and sponge the surface of all the sugarpaste (page 25). Leave to dry.

4 Make the drapes and bows in strengthened sugarpaste as shown left, and attach to the cake. Cut two hearts from white sugarpaste and glue in position in the centre of the cake. Attach smaller hearts around the base. Add piped dots and two royal icing doves, if wished.

Frilling

Frilling has become a very popular decorative technique that works well with sugarpaste. A variety of frill cutters is available, round and straight, with a choice of edges. We have started with the original, the Garrett frill cutter (named after Elaine Garrett who first developed the technique).

If your sugarpaste is quite soft you might need to strengthen it, either by adding 1 teaspoon gum tragacanth to every 450g (1lb) sugarpaste, or by making up a different paste that is 75 per cent sugarpaste and 25 per cent flower paste (page 84).

1 Using a paper template and a scriber, mark a line on the side of the cake along which the frills will be positioned.

EXPERT ADVICE

When dusting with cornflour, use a muslin bag to ensure an even and thin distribution of the cornflour.

2 Roll out the paste thinly on a non-stick board dusted with a small amount of cornflour.

3 Cut out a frill with a Garrett frill cutter. Carefully remove the cut-out centre of the frill.

4 Bring the frill to the edge of the board, ensuring that it slides easily. Frill the edges with a cocktail stick (toothpick), using the side of the stick and not the point to avoid making marks. Holding the stick with one hand and using the pres-

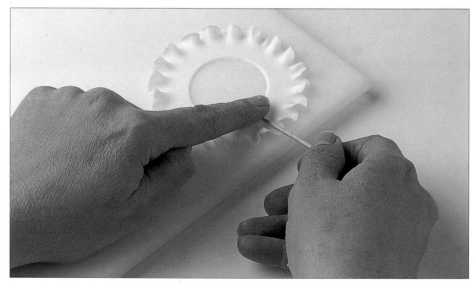

sure of the forefinger of the other hand, continue to roll and frill all the way around, turning the frill as you go. Work quickly so that the edge of the frill does not dry out and start to break.

5 Cut through the frill to make one long strip, and turn it over. Paint some cool boiled water along the unfrilled, flat edge.

6 Lift the frill with both hands and line up the unfrilled edge along the marked line on the cake. Cut the frill to the correct size with a scalpel, small sharp knife or fine scissors. Ease gently into position. Use a cocktail stick to turn the ends of the frill under, allowing the frill to roll around the stick, until the stick is at right angles to the cake.

7 Again with the help of the cocktail stick or your fingers, lift all the pleats in the frill until the overall effect is evenly distributed.

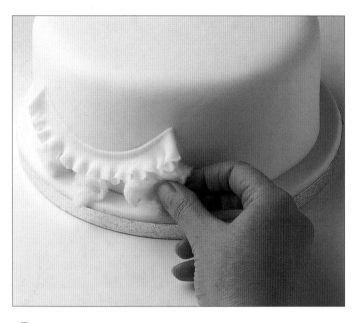

8   Alternatively, support the frill with some cotton wool or tiny pieces of foam, until dry. To complete, neaten the top edge of the frill with a knife or scalpel.

9   For double frills, apply the bottom layer first (which can be a different colour from the cake), lining up the top edge of the frill to just below the marked line on the cake. Leave this layer to firm up before applying the second frill, lining the top of this one up with just above the marked line on the cake. Turn the cut edges under.

10   For a pierced double frill, apply the first layer of frills and leave them to firm up. Cut frills for the second layer in a contrasting colour. After frilling the edge, but before cutting through the frill, use the smallest plunger cutter to cut out evenly spaced shapes just above the frilled area. Apply to the cake. Decorate the top edge of the frill with small plunger cutter flowers cut from the paste used for the under-frill, attaching with a little cool boiled water.

11   The top edge can also be neatened with piped bulbs or shells,

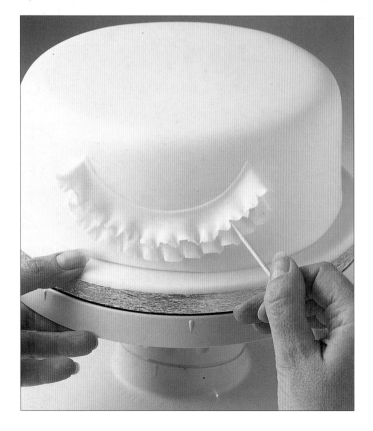

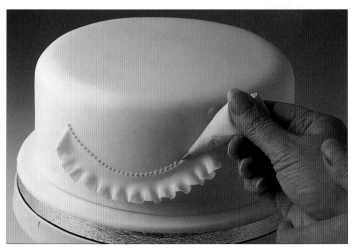

using a no. 1 or no. 2 tube (tip) and royal icing (page 54). Try using different colours.

12 Although more time-consuming, a picot edge can look very attractive. With a no. 1 tube and royal icing, pipe small bulbs in sets of three along the top edge of all the frills on the cake, then add two bulbs nestling in the gaps between the first three bulbs. Finally, add a single bulb on top of the two piped previously. As an alternative, try using different shades of the same colour icing, starting with a dark colour and lightening it by adding more white royal icing for each layer.

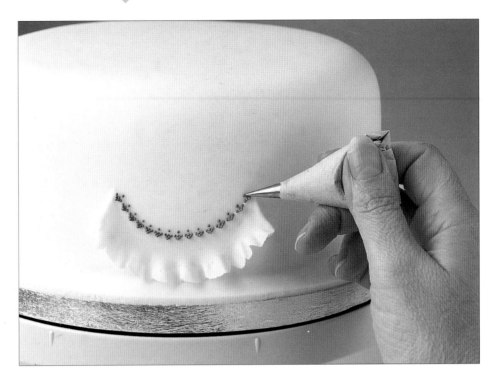

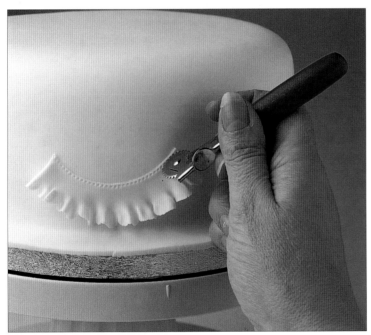

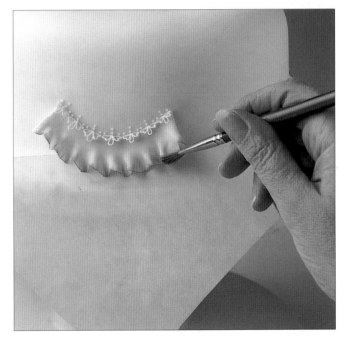

13 A tailor's wheel can be rolled along the soft top edge of the frills to give a stitched effect. Try two or even three rows as an alternative.

14 A dusting of colour makes an attractive finish to frills. Slide some greaseproof paper under the frill to protect the bottom of the cake and the coated cake drum. Work powder food colouring (petal dust/blossom tint) into the side of a flat brush and gently stroke the brush upwards across the bottom of the frill. This will produce a strongly coloured edge and a fading out of colour upwards. The top edge of the frill can be finished with lace (page 70).

EXPERT ADVICE

To obtain a softer coloured edge to your frill, mix the petal dust with cornflour to weaken the colour. Lustre powders give a pretty effect.

BRODERIE ANGLAISE

This technique is used on sugarpaste which is still soft. Impressions made in the sugarpaste become part of the finished design.

1 Trace the pattern (page 134) on to greaseproof paper and place in position on the cake surface. Mark the main points of the pattern through to the cake surface with a scriber. Remove the pattern and enlarge the main holes with a modelling tool or clean knitting needle.

3 Different-coloured icing can be used to complete the piping.

APPLIED BRODERIE ANGLAISE

Broderie anglaise can also be made in pieces and applied to the cake.

template and scalpel or a broderie anglaise cutter. Frill the edge, if required (page 38). Cut a pattern of small holes using no. 3 and no. 2 piping tubes (tips) to obtain different-sized holes.

2 Moisten the top edge of the shape with cool boiled water, and

2 Pipe around the holes with royal icing and a no. 0 tube (tip), imitating the machine-stitched designs of fabric broderie anglaise.

1 Roll out sugarpaste and cut out the shape required, using either a

with the flat of your hand or an icing polisher to create a smooth surface.

3 Use a rolling pin to lift the paste and lower it into position on the top of the cake. *Do not* moisten the surface of the cake. Remove the rolling pin and adjust the cloth so that it sits evenly on the top of the cake.

4 Create even folds around the edge with your fingers, and leave to dry. A 'tablecloth' can be added to round or square cakes, with or without a patterned edge. On a square cake, the points of the square 'cloth' should hang in the middle of the sides for a neat finish.

glue the shape to the cake. Ease the frills into shape with fingertips.

3 Complete the design by piping the 'stitched' pattern in royal icing with a no. 0 tube.

'TABLECLOTH'

A variety of interesting effects can be created by laying a second thin coat of sugarpaste over the cake, and shaping it to resemble a cloth draped over. The base coat of sugarpaste can be thinner than usual as an extra layer is applied.

1 Measure the diameter of the coated cake. Add 7.5cm (3 inches) to this measurement and make a paper template. Make up a paste composed of 25 per cent flower paste (page 84) and 75 per cent sugarpaste, kneading well to make a paste with a firmer consistency.

2 Roll out the paste as thinly as possible on a non-stick board. Hold the template lightly on the surface and cut round the template with a sharp knife. Remove the template and polish the surface of the paste

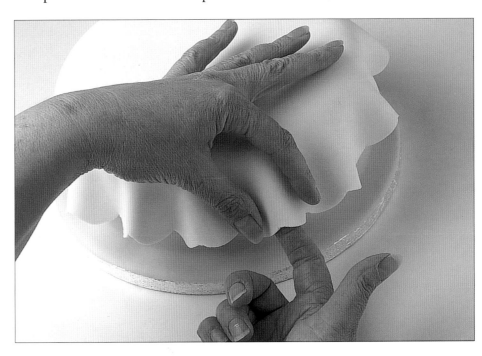

Rag Doll Cake

MATERIALS
15cm (6 inch) round cake
Apricot glaze (page 13)
450g (1lb) marzipan (almond paste)
900g (2lb) sugarpaste
Selection of food colourings
28cm (11 inch) round cake drum
Small amount of royal icing
100g (4oz) flower paste
Clear alcohol (gin or vodka)
Ribbon to trim cake drum

EQUIPMENT
Icing polishers
Scriber
Broderie anglaise cutters or
templates (page 134)
Piping bags
Nos. 0, 1, 2 and 3 piping tubes (tips)

1 Brush the cake with apricot glaze, and coat with marzipan using the all-in-one method (page 13). Coat the cake with pink sugarpaste, trimming neatly at the base of the cake (page 20). Trace the top design (page 134) and scribe on to the top of the cake. Leave to dry.

2 Coat the cake drum in white sugarpaste. Make a petal-shaped template from a 25cm (10 inch) circle of greaseproof paper. Make a second template the size of the coated cake. Brush the outside edge only of the white sugarpaste on the drum with cool boiled water, and coat the drum again in pink sugarpaste.

3 Place the petal-shaped template slightly off centre on the pink sugarpaste and cut around it with a pointed knife, cutting through the pink paste only. Hold the template in position with the minimum of pressure to ensure that the two layers of sugarpaste do not stick together. Lift out the central part of the pink sugarpaste and smooth the cut edge with your fingertips.

4 Place the cake-sized template on the coated drum, again off centre, and cut around it. Lift out the unwanted sugarpaste. Lower the cake into position, directly on to the surface of the cake drum, and smooth the cut edge of the soft sugarpaste on the board to neaten the join. Pipe a snailstrail around the base of the cake in royal icing with a no. 1 tube.

5 Trace the broderie anglaise pattern from the centre of the side and board design (page 134), turn (top to bottom) and scribe on to the pink paste on the drum.

6 Make the applied broderie anglaise pieces from white sugarpaste (page 42), using the side design template on page 134, and apply to the cake, smoothing the top cut edges with your fingertips.

7 Pipe all the broderie anglaise patterns in royal icing with a no. 0 tube.

8 Make lace (page 70), and leave to dry.

9 The rag doll is made from a half and half mixture of flower paste and sugarpaste. Make a pear shape for the body and a ball for the head, and flatten both pieces. Make two sausages for the legs. Place the pear shape in position beside the cake. Shape the legs and feet, and make, or paint on, shoes. Place in position. Dress the body with a piece of applied broderie anglaise (page 42). Make the arms from sausage shapes, shape and glue in position. Cut a bodice in pink, and glue over the body and top of the arms. Paint the face and leave to dry before gluing the head in position. Add hair made by the ropes and plaits method (page 35). Add a bonnet and bow (page 36).

10 To complete the cake, attach the lace (page 70) and add a ribbon to the edge of the cake drum.

STENCILLING

This technique can be applied direct to the finished surface of a cake or to separate cut pieces of sugarpaste. The stencilling can be transferred in powder colours or royal icing, as shown here, but can also be sprayed through with an airbrush, or sponged with liquid colours or paste colours mixed with alcohol (page 25).

POWDER COLOUR STENCILLING

1   Make up a half-and-half mixture of flower paste (page 84) and sugarpaste, and roll out thinly on a non-stick board. Rub a little white vegetable fat (shortening) over the surface of the paste and lay the stencil on. Smooth down well with the side of your hand.

2   Choose some dusting powders (petal dusts/blossom tints) and a flat brush, and, starting with the lightest colour, dust the open cut areas to the strength required. Blow away any loose dust and carefully peel the stencil away from the paste.

3   Cut around the design, if required, using a scalpel, and lift carefully into position.

ROYAL ICING STENCILLING

1   Lay the stencil on the surface of the cake, which can be coated in royal icing, marzipan or sugarpaste.

2   Place a little royal icing on an icing palette and paddle smooth, adding colour if required. Ensure that the royal icing is at a firm peak consistency (page 51). Use a cranked palette knife to smooth the royal icing across the stencil area. Carefully peel the stencil away. Leave to dry.

3   Paint or pipe details on to the stencilled design.

Honeysuckle Stencil Cake

MATERIALS
20cm (8 inch) round cake
Apricot glaze (page 13)
900g (2lb) marzipan (almond paste)
25cm (10 inch) round cake drum
900g (2lb) sugarpaste
100g (4oz) flower paste (page 84)
White vegetable fat (shortening)
Selection of powder food colourings
Ribbon to trim cake drum

EQUIPMENT
Stencils (e.g. Sarah Gleave's honeysuckle and striped stencils)
Flat dusting brushes

1   Brush the cake with apricot glaze and coat in marzipan using the all-in-one method (page 13).

2   Place the cake on the cake drum. Brush the marzipan with cool boiled water and coat the cake and board with sugarpaste (page 22). Leave to dry.

3   Make up a half-and-half mixture of sugarpaste and flower paste, roll out and stencil as described (left). Cut out the stencil and position on the top of the cake.

4   Repeat the technique for the band around the side of the cake. The striped stencil design needs to be repeated approximately two and a half times to fit around this size of cake; you will find it easier to apply in short pieces rather than one long strip.

5   Colour a piece of the mixed flower/sugarpaste green and roll out to 2.5mm (⅛ inch) thick. Cut a 1cm (½ inch) strip and attach to the bottom edge of the striped border. Trim the cake drum with ribbon.

PIPING WITH JELLY

Clear piping jelly can be coloured to create bright pictures on cakes coated in sugarpaste. The glossy surface of the jelly does not go cloudy as it dries.

1 While the sugarpaste is still soft, emboss it with the design (page 135) as described on page 73. Pipe the outlines using melted chocolate with a little glycerine added (page 128). Leave to set.

2 Colour piping jelly as required and put into paper piping bags. Snip the tips off the bags and pipe the jelly into the various areas of the design.

Matchstick People Cake

MATERIALS
Genoese or Victoria sandwich cake (pages 9–10), trimmed to 15x23cm (6x9 inches)
Apricot glaze (page 13)
450g (1lb) marzipan (almond paste)
20x30cm (8x12 inch) rectangular cake drum
450g (1lb) sugarpaste
50g (2oz) plain chocolate, melted
A few drops of glycerine
100g (4oz) piping jelly
Selection of food colourings
Small amount of royal icing
Ribbon to trim cake drum

EQUIPMENT
Icing polishers
Piping bags
No. 42 or 44 piping tube (tip)

1 Brush the cake with apricot glaze, and coat with marzipan using the all-in-one method (page 13).

2 Position the cake on the cake drum. Brush the marzipan with cool boiled water, and coat the cake and drum in sugarpaste (page 22). Leave to set for 5 minutes.

3 Transfer the design (page 135) to the freshly sugarpasted surface of the cake, using the embossing method (page 73). Pipe the outlines in piping chocolate (page 128). Fill in the shapes using coloured piping jelly, as described left.

4 Pipe a shell border in royal icing, using a no. 42 or 44 tube, (page 58) and trim the edge of the cake drum with ribbon.

ROYAL ICING

Often spoken of as the 'master medium', royal icing gives a beautiful finish to a cake and can be used in any number of decorative ways, from simple piping and linework to brush embroidery, runout designs and piped bridge and extension work. Some of the most attractive cake decorations are made with royal icing using different piping techniques, including delicate lace work and lettering. Knowing how to make the best royal icing for the technique you are practising will give you confidence and help you produce the best possible results.

MAKING ROYAL ICING

It is as well to remember that the finer the work, the stronger the royal icing needs to be. Stronger icing is made, not necessarily by using a thicker mixture, but by varying the ingredients.

Icing (confectioners') sugar used for royal icing should be fine and should not need to be sifted before use. For very fine piping work, it is possible to buy 'superfine' icing sugar. If you cannot obtain this, it is better to sieve royal icing after it has been made through a piece of muslin (or a clean piece of an old pair of tights or a stocking).

You can make royal icing in any quantity, depending on whether you need it for coating a large cake or for a small amount of decorative piping. As a quick guide, for all quantities, combine 1 measure of albumen solution to 5½ of icing sugar.

TYPES OF ALBUMEN

PURE ALBUMEN This is available in powder form and is pure pasteurized hen albumen. It is reconstituted with water. Use pure albumen in royal icing which needs to have a lot of strength, i.e. for making runouts, lace, extension work or any prefabricated off-pieces.

ALBUMEN SUBSTITUTE This is also available in powder form and, depending upon the manufacturer, will be composed of additives mixed with a small amount of pure albumen. The additives generally are either milk-powder-based or alginate-based. This produces a slightly softer-setting royal icing which is ideal for coating and general piping.

FRESH EGG WHITE This is ideal for small amounts of royal icing when you may not wish to reconstitute powders. Choose the freshest eggs possible, and ensure that no yolk at all mixes with the egg white. Always weigh the egg white before mixing.

PREPARING ALBUMEN SOLUTION

If using pure albumen, mix 1 part powder with 7 parts warm water, cover with clingfilm (plastic wrap) and leave to soften in the refrigerator for 1 hour. (Alternatively, use cold water and leave to soak overnight in the refrigerator.) If using albumen substitute, whisk 1 part powder into 10 parts cold water. This can be used immediately.

1 Measure 150ml (¼ pint) water into a bowl and whisk in 20g (¾ oz) pure albumen powder using a fork or small balloon whisk. The mixture will go lumpy. Cover with clingfilm, place in the refrigerator, and leave to soften.

2 Remove from the refrigerator and whisk again. Strain the albumen solution through a fine sieve or

clean tea strainer into a clean, grease-free bowl that is large enough for making the royal icing.

Royal Icing

Makes enough to coat and pipe an average 18–20cm (7–8 inch) cake.

20g (¾ oz) albumen powder
150ml (¼ pint / ⅔ cup) water
1kg (2¼ lb) icing (confectioners') sugar

1 Make up the albumen solution as described left, and sieve into a clean, grease-free bowl. Weigh and sift the icing sugar, and add one third to the albumen solution. Beat on the lowest speed, using a hand-held electric mixer. Add another third of the icing sugar and beat again on slow speed.

BROOKLANDS COLLEGE LIBRARY
WEYBRIDGE, SURREY KT13 8TT

COATING WITH ROYAL ICING

2 Add the remaining icing sugar in small portions, still beating on slow speed.

3 Continue beating on slow speed until the icing reaches a 'firm peak' consistency. Clean down the sides of the bowl and beater, and cover with a clean damp cloth until required. Alternatively, place the royal icing in a lidded plastic container until required.

VARIATION

For a softer cutting icing, add 1–3 teaspoons glycerine to 450g (1lb) royal icing. For a single-tier cake, add 3 teaspoons glycerine; for tiered cakes add 1–2 teaspoons glycerine.

To make a stronger setting royal icing, add acetic acid or lemon juice; the acid helps to strengthen the albumen.

Royal icing has long been considered the traditional coating for formal celebration cakes. It provides a smooth, firm surface with sharply angled corners and edges. Coating with royal icing is, however, time-consuming as the icing has to be applied in several coats, and each coat must be left to dry before the next coat can be applied. Before coating with royal icing, cover the cake with marzipan using the top and sides method described on page 14, and leave to dry for 24 hours. An icing turntable is necessary when coating a cake with royal icing.

ROUND CAKE

1 The consistency of the royal icing required for the first and second coats should be 'soft peak'. This might mean adding a little water to the royal icing. If the icing has been left to stand for a while, stir gently before use.

2 Place the cake on a turntable. Place a small amount of royal icing in the centre of the cake and, using a backwards and forwards motion (as if spreading butter on bread), and keeping the palette knife reasonably flat, smooth the icing over the surface of the cake. Continue in

this way until you have covered the whole top surface of the cake, keeping the palette knife in one general position and turning the turntable for an even coating.

3 To obtain a more even surface, make a 360° sweep. This is achieved by holding the tip of the palette knife in the centre of the cake with the blade across the radius angled at 10°. Turn the cake a full 360° into the open angle of the knife.

EXPERT ADVICE

The amount of icing first placed on the surface of the cake is generally about twice the amount needed. At least half the icing is removed during the smoothing process.

4 Anchor the turntable to prevent it moving, or place the cake on a barely damp cloth on a flat surface (so that it doesn't slide). Wipe an icing ruler with a damp cloth, and place the ruler on the far edge of the cake, holding the ends of the ruler with both hands, thumbs uppermost. Angle the ruler at 10° to the surface of the cake, drag it quickly towards the near side of the cake, and pull off. Wipe the ruler clean. If there are any obvious marks in the icing, repeat the process, cleaning the ruler between each attempt. This action should be completed swiftly; pulling the ruler slowly across will result in fine, wavy lines.

5 Remove the surplus icing from the edge of the cake by holding the palette knife parallel with the side of the cake and pushing downwards with a cutting action. Lift off small amounts of royal icing at a time, cleaning the knife as you go. Leave

until dry; the time needed will vary depending on the thickness of the coat, the room temperature, humidity, etc. When dry, the icing will have a matte finish and will feel dry to the touch.

6 To coat the side of the cake, take small amounts of royal icing on the tip of the palette knife and apply to the bottom edge. Use the same paddling action as you used for the top of the cake to spread the icing from the bottom edge up the side of the cake. Note how the palette knife is held parallel to the cake side. Continue until the side of the cake is covered all round.

7 Wipe a side scraper with a damp cloth. To hold the scraper, spread your fingers evenly over the back of it and use the pad of your little finger to lift the scraper away from the cake drum slightly. Place the scraper at a 30° angle to the side of the cake, press it into the soft sugar, and turn

the cake on the turntable through 360°, keeping the side scraper in the same position.

8 If there are any obvious faults or marks in the coating, repeat the process, wiping the scraper between each attempt.

9 For an interesting alternative to a plain, smooth finish to the cake sides, a patterned scraper is effective.

10 Use the palette knife to clean away excess royal icing from the top edge of the cake, cutting towards the centre of the cake and keeping the palette knife nearly flat on the surface. Leave to dry.

11 When the icing is dry, remove any rough edges, and particularly the 'take off' mark, with a sharp knife and a scraping action.

12 Use a soft, dry brush to remove surplus sugar dust created by the scraping action of the knife.

13 Repeat steps 1–12 to give a second coat. Leave to dry.

14 For the final coat, soften the royal icing down a little more with water. Alternatively, use 'matured' royal icing (this is icing that has been kept for at least three days, has absorbed moisture from the damp cloth covering it, and has been stirred each day).

15 Coat the board by paddling small amounts of royal icing on to it with the tip of the palette knife.

16 Use the palette knife at a 10° angle to smooth the icing on the board, again making a single 360° sweep. Clean off the board edge with the palette knife using a cutting down action and removing small amounts at a time. Clean the knife between each action. Wipe the edge of the cake drum clean with a damp cloth. Leave to dry.

SQUARE CAKE

1 A slightly different action is necessary to coat the sides of a square cake. Apply the icing as for a round cake, with a paddling action.

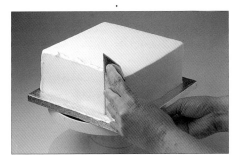

Place the side scraper at the far corner of the side coated and at a 30° angle. Hold the turntable still and pull the scraper in one action across the side of the cake. Repeat if necessary, cleaning the scraper.

2 Once a smooth side coat is achieved, clean off the top and side edges with the palette knife, using the cutting action shown for a round cake. Repeat on the opposite side of the cake and leave to dry before coating the two alternate sides.

SPONGING WITH ROYAL ICING

One example of an attractive but simple way to finish a cake that has been coated in royal icing or sugarpaste, is to sponge the surface with royal icing. Mix some royal icing on a palette with a little water to soften, and colour if required. Using a piece of open-textured sponge, texture the surface of the cake with the royal icing.

PIPING WITH ROYAL ICING

Piped royal icing adds a very professional touch to any cake, whether it is used to create simple lines and scrolls, or combined with other techniques to add colourful and eye-catching designs. Royal icing is usually piped using greaseproof paper piping bags, with or without a piping tube (tip). Perfect piping demands a steady hand and plenty of practice, but the results are always worth the time taken.

PIPING BAGS

Greaseproof paper is usually sold in rectangular sheets, so it makes sense to cut triangles for the piping bags from this shape, rather than to trim the paper into squares. This has the added advantage of strengthening the back join when folded, where there will be three layers of paper instead of two.

1 Fold one short side of a rectangular sheet of greaseproof paper over and across one long side, overlapping the long side by about 5cm (2 inches). Cut through the folded edge with a sharp knife, producing two equal-sized triangles, each with one blunt corner.

2 Hold the blunt corner of one triangle in your writing hand. With your other hand, find the central point on the longest edge and place your index finger at this point. Turn the paper once only, creating a point at the centre point marked by your finger.

3 Lift the cone and wrap the far corner of the paper once around it, bringing all the points of the triangle together at the back.

4 Adjust the tightness of the cone by moving the three corners, checking the base forms a tight point.

5 Fold over all three points *at least twice* to create a good seal at the top of the piping bag.

6 Prepare the royal icing by paddling it smooth on an icing palette.

7 Fill the bag half to two-thirds full with royal icing. Do not overfill the bag! Use the thumb hole in the icing palette (or something similar) to hold the bag while you fill it.

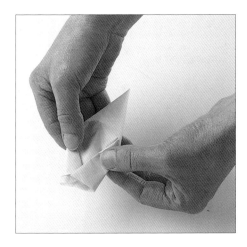

8 Seal the piping bag by first folding in the sides, keeping the top of the bag straight.

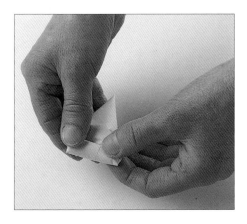

9 Fold down the top of the bag, until you cannot fold it any more.

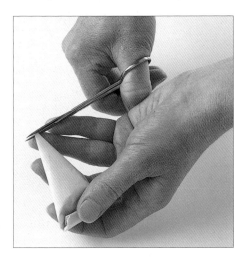

10 To pipe without a piping tube (tip), the bag is now ready to

be cut. Cut straight across for piping lines and simple writing.

11 For italic (script) writing and piping small petals and leaves, cut the bag at an angle.

12 Make a second angled cut in the opposite direction for piping larger leaves with a central vein.

USING PIPING TUBES

Piping tubes (tips) are available in a huge range of sizes, both plain and shaped for special purposes. Once you have made a piping bag, cut a large hole in the tip, and drop in the tube before filling with royal icing.

PIPING STRAIGHT LINES Fit a piping bag with a small plain tube (tip) and fill with royal icing.

1 Touch the tube down on to the surface, and start squeezing the bag.

2 Lift the tube, allowing icing to extrude in a straight line. To help keep the line straight, stretch the sugar slightly, still squeezing.

3. As the end of the line is almost reached, lower the tube to the surface, easing off the pressure. Touch the tube down, stop squeezing, and lift off.

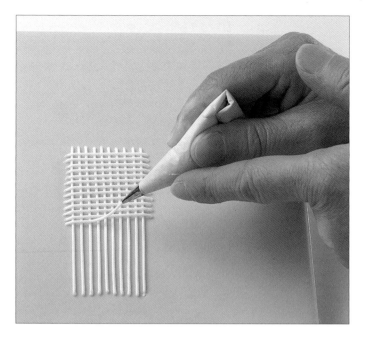

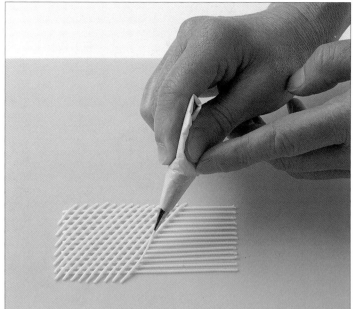

SQUARE TRELLIS This is a good technique for practising piping straight lines, and is excellent for covering designated areas of cake. Pipe parallel lines in one direction, then pipe another set of parallel lines at 90° to the first. Pipe the lines close together but not touching.

DIAMOND TRELLIS This alternative to square trellis piping (left) involves piping a set of parallel lines first, then piping a second set of parallel lines at an angle of 45° to the first.

CORNELLI Use this piping technique to cover areas of cake. Pipe a series of wiggly 'M' and 'W' lines with a no. 1 or no. 0 tube (tip), without allowing the lines to touch each other.

FILIGREE This is similar to cornelli work, but for piped filigree the wiggly 'M' and 'W' lines should be finer (use a no. 0 tube), and should touch each other to form a solid shape. This technique is often used for royal-iced off-pieces as well as for piping directly on to a cake.

LINEWORK

Lines piped using graduated sizes of tubes (tips) and built up one on top of the other, and one inside the other, create a neat border or framing effect.

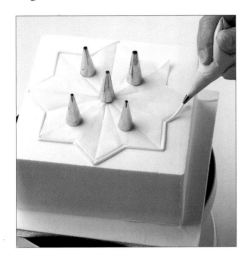

1 Linework is easier to pipe if you prepare a template to follow (page 135). The template can be held in position with a few spare piping tubes. Pipe the thickest line first with a plain no. 3 tube. Remove the template.

2 Pipe a line with a no. 2 tube alongside the first line (this can be inside or outside the first line, depending upon your design). Pipe a no. 2 line on top of the no. 3 line.

3 Using a no. 1 tube, pipe a line alongside the no. 2 line, and on top of both no. 2 lines (the single no. 2 line and the no. 2 line piped on top of the no. 3 line).

PIPING WITH CUT TUBES

COARSE-CUT TUBES (TIPS) These are generally used for piping large royal icing shapes and buttercream. The illustration (below) shows

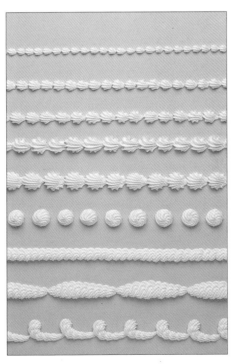

EXPERT ADVICE

As you become more practised at linework, reduce the tube (tip) sizes to nos. 2, 1 and 0.

shells piped with tube nos. 5, 6, 7, 8 and 13 (top 5 rows). Row 6 shows rosettes, row 7 continuous rope, row 8 graduated rope, and row 9 'C' scrolls (see pages 58–60).

FINE-CUT TUBES (TIPS) These give a more refined finish. The top three rows of piping (above) show shell piping, piped with tube nos. 42, 43 and 44. Row 4 shows continuous rope, row 5 graduated rope with overpiping, row 6 'C' scrolls with overpiping, row 7 'S' scrolls with overpiping, row 8 'S' and 'C' scrolls with overpiping, and row 9 mirror image 'S' and 'C' scrolls with overpiping (see pages 58–60).

PIPING SHELLS

Use a star tube (tip) of a suitable size (usually no. 42, 43 or 44, depending on the size of the cake). Position the bag at an angle of 45° to the cake and pipe a bulb shape. Whilst pulling back, gradually decrease the pressure on the bag until a point is formed at the far end of the shell. Continue in this way until your design is complete. Shells may be overpiped. Here are some examples:

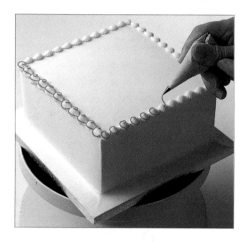

SIMPLE 'C' OVERPIPING Use a no. 1 tube to create a 'C' shape over each shell. Start from the centre of the shell and lift the icing, forming a 'C' shape over the top of the shell, around the outside edge and finishing at the point.

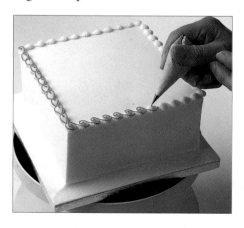

'S' SHAPE OVERPIPING Starting from the centre of one shell, lift the

icing around the back of the shell, and bring the line of piping across the point of the first shell and over to the front of the second shell, ending at the point of the second shell.

OVERPIPING WITH LOOPS Start piping at the point of one shell, lift the icing across the front of the shell and touch down at the point of the next shell.

'S' SCROLL PIPING

To pipe the 'S' scroll, use a star tube of a suitable size (usually no. 42, 43 or 44). Start with strong pressure and rotate the tube towards the centre of the cake, in an up-and-over motion. Decrease the pressure to form the back of the scroll, finishing by pulling the icing into a tail. The scroll design can be varied in the following ways:

OVERPIPING Overpipe 'S' scrolls first with a no. 42 tube held at an angle of 70° to the cake, pushing the icing into the scroll to fill any gaps

in the rope pattern, and to create a smooth base for 3-2-1 overpiping.

LINKED SCROLLS Repeat the 'S' shape, this time taking the tail of the scroll over the edge of the cake. Tuck the second 'S' scroll behind the tail

of the first, thereby creating a linked effect. Overpipe using nos. 42, 3, 2 and 1 tubes.

ing the line of icing. Build up pressure on the bag when piping the centre of each section, then decrease the pressure to the side.

'S' SCROLL OVERPIPING Pipe an 'S' scroll on top of each section of graduated rope, then overpipe using nos. 42, 3, 2 and 1 tubes.

'C' SCROLLS These scrolls are piped in a letter 'C' shape, starting with a bulb and rotating the tube outwards. Decrease the pressure on the bag to produce a fine tail.

OVERPIPING WITH LOOPS Overpipe the graduated rope with 3-2-1 loops.

'S' AND 'C' SCROLL OVERPIPING Pipe 'S' and 'C' scrolls on top of each section of graduated rope, then overpipe using nos. 42, 3, 2 and 1 tubes.

'S' AND 'C' SCROLLS A further pattern is developed by piping 'S' and 'C' scrolls together. The 'S' and 'C' should touch tails to produce a slender finish.

GRADUATED ROPE

The graduated rope design can be used around the top and bottom edge of a cake, and overpiped in various ways. Divide the edge of the cake into equal sections. Using a star tube (tip) and a small amount of pressure, pipe graduated rope piping between the divisions, rotat-

MIRROR IMAGE PIPING

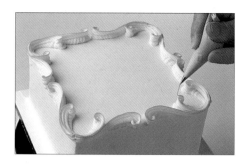

'S' AND 'C' TO CORNER To build up shape in the centre of each side of a square cake, pipe 'S' and 'C' scrolls from the centre point, graduating the tails down at the corners of the cake. Overpipe using nos. 42, 3, 2 and 1 tubes, to finish.

'S' AND 'C' TO SIDES To make the corners of a square cake appear larger, start the 'S' and 'C' scroll pattern at that point, graduating the tails down to the centre of each side.

DOUBLE 'S' AND 'C' An even bolder design is produced by piping two 'S' scrolls, one slightly larger than the other, and then adding a 'C' scroll, and overpiping as before.

Lily-of-the-Valley Cake

MATERIALS
20x15cm (8x6 inch) oval cake
Apricot glaze (page 13)
900g (2lb) marzipan (almond paste)
25x20cm (10x8 inch) oval cake drum
Royal icing made with albumen substitute
(page 50)
Green food colouring
Ribbon to trim cake drum

EQUIPMENT
Icing ruler
Side scraper
Piping bags
Nos. 0, 1, 2, 3, 42 and 44 piping tubes (tips)

1 Brush the cake with apricot glaze, and coat in marzipan using the top and sides method on page 14. Leave to dry.

2 Apply three layers of royal icing, leaving to dry between coats (page 51). Coat the board (page 53) and leave to dry.

3 Trace the top design template (page 137) on to greaseproof paper, cut out and secure in position on top of the cake. Pipe 3-2-1 linework around the edge of the template (page 57). Remove the template.

4 Following the curves of the linework, pipe one large 'S' and two 'C' scrolls with a no. 44 tube (page 58). Following the remaining curve, pipe a row of shells with a no. 44 tube (page 58) along the opposite edge of the cake.

5 Pipe the mirrored pattern on the base edge of the cake and board with a no. 44 tube.

6 Overpipe the 'S' and 'C' scrolls with a no. 42 tube, holding the tube in a vertical position and pressing very slightly on to the scroll shapes to fill in any gaps and produce a flat surface for overpiping.

7 Overpipe the shells and scrolls with 3-2-1 linework (page 57). Side linework may also be piped if required. To make piping on the side of the cake easier, place a solid, flat object under the edge of the front of the board to tilt the side upwards and provide a flatter surface to pipe on to.

8 Complete the design with green stems and leaves, piped following the shape of the template. (Trace and scribe the designs on page 137 for guidance, if required.) Pipe small lily-of-the-valley directly on to the cake (page 63), and graduated bulbs to finish the design on the top and sides of the cake.

9 To finish, attach a ribbon to the edge of the cake drum (see Expert Advice, below).

EXPERT ADVICE

When attaching ribbon to the edge of a cake drum or board, the best method is to apply double-sided sticky tape to the board before attaching the ribbon. Alternatively, use an ordinary glue stick (e.g. Pritt). Do not use royal icing as the ribbon will fall away when the icing dries.

DIRECT PIPED TECHNIQUES

As well as the classical piping described on pages 54–60, there are a number of other ways in which patterns and designs can be piped directly on to a prepared cake.

EXTENSION WORK

Extension work consists of parallel lines of royal icing piped from the cake's surface to a 'bridge' of piping already constructed on the cake. There are two basic shapes of bridgework: the first is built up by piping continuous loops of the same size directly on top of each other; the second starts with small loops, which are overpiped with longer loops, increasing in length.

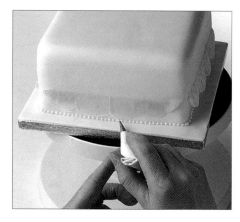

1 Make a paper pattern for the shape of the bridgework, ensuring that the pattern will fit evenly in the space allowed (e.g. along one side of a cake). Tilt the cake away from you. Pipe the first line of bridgework directly under the paper pattern with a no. 1 tube (tip). Mark the top edge of the extension work with a scriber. Remove the template and continue building up loops until the required depth is obtained (approximately 7–8 layers).

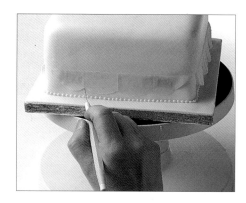

2 Alternatively, mark the pattern for the bridgework and the top of the extension work with a scriber, and remove the paper template before you begin piping.

3 Pipe the first loop in the centre of each division, approximately 2.5mm (⅛ inch) long. Repeat this for all divisions. Pipe the second loop directly on top of the first loop but a little longer in length. Continue to repeat this build-up until the loops are complete and the sections of bridgework are touching. If a deeper effect is required, continue building up loops as in step 1, left. To fill the little gaps that this produces, mix a little royal icing with water to produce a soft medium and paint this over the bridgework. For a different effect, this mixture can be coloured.

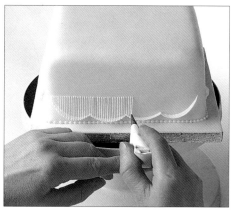

4 Using a no. 1 or no. 0 tube, pipe parallel lines from the top scribed line to the bridge. These lines should be straight and close enough together not to allow another line to be piped between them. Straight and even lines will be achieved by tilting the top of the cake slightly towards you, allowing gravity to pull the icing line directly perpendicular. Take care not to stretch the icing as you pipe as this will cause the line to break or look uneven. When each line is complete, stop squeezing and carefully lower the tube underneath the bridge to break the flow of icing from the tube.

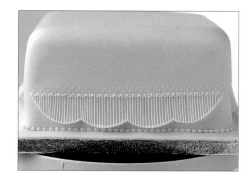

5 The top edge of the extension work can be neatened by a variety of methods. One such method is to pipe a small, even row of loops con-

cealing the tops of the extension lines. This can be finished with piped dots.

6 An alternative finishing technique is to attach sugar lace across the top edge (page 70).

TUBE EMBROIDERY

Using a fine piping tube (tip) and royal icing as a needle and thread, many embroidery patterns can be transferred on to cakes.

1 Trace the pattern (page 133) on to greaseproof paper. Place in position on the cake and mark the main features of the pattern using a scriber.

2 Using a no. 1 or no. 0 tube, pipe over the scribed lines and dots.

3 A variety of embroidered flowers and stems are simple to pipe directly on to the cake's surface: the yellow flowers illustrated are made from a circle of five dots; the pink flowers are circles of five or six shells with their points towards a dot of yellow in the centre; the blue flowers consist of three shells with their points going outwards (see Lily-of-the-Valley Cake, page 60); the purple flowers are made up of two rows of dots either side of the stem, followed by a row of dots piped on top of the stem.

DIRECT PIPED PICTURES

This is a quick and simple way of transferring a design using piped lines. Transfer the traced design through the greaseproof paper on to the cake with a scriber.

DANCERS This design (page 137) illustrates the way in which simple

piped lines can be used to express shading as well as basic outlines.

FAIRY This design (page 135) is first piped in various colours, and then enhanced with coloured dusts and liquid food colourings.

Wedding Cake

MATERIALS

15cm (6 inch), 20cm (8 inch) and 25cm
(10 inch) round fruit cakes
Apricot glaze (page 13)
3kg (6½lb) marzipan (almond paste)
2.5kg (5½lb) royal icing made with
albumen substitute (page 50), for coating
and piping
Cream paste food colouring
20cm (8 inch), 25cm (10 inch) and 33cm
(13 inch) round cake drums
Ice blue and mint green paste food
colourings
450g (1lb) royal icing made with pure
albumen (page 50), for runouts, lace and
extension work
Ribbon to trim cake drums

EQUIPMENT

Icing ruler
Side scraper
Piping bags
Nos. 1, 2 and 3 piping tubes (tips)
Piece of sponge
Cake separators or pillars

1 Brush the cakes with apricot glaze, and coat in marzipan using the top and sides method on page 14. Leave to dry.

2 Coat the cakes with three layers of royal icing coloured light cream, leaving each coat to dry before applying the next (page 51). Place the cakes on the cake drums, and coat the drums around the cakes with cream royal icing (page 53).

3 Trace and cut out loop templates (page 139), and pipe the linework in cream royal icing with a no. 3 tube following the templates, as shown on page 57. Continue the linework down the sides and across the board of each cake. Following the technique described on page 53,

sponge the space inside the panels with royal icing coloured with a mixture of ice blue and mint green. Finish the linework with no. 2 and no. 1 tubes.

4 Pipe bulbs along the bottom edge of each cake, in between the panels, with cream royal icing and a no. 3 tube. Pipe bulbs along the top edge with a no. 2 tube.

5 Using cream royal icing, pipe on the bridgework for the extension lines and, when dry, pipe in the extension lines (page 62).

6 Make the lace on waxed paper (pages 70 and 139), having coloured the icing with a mixture of ice blue and mint green.

7 Produce two runouts of the top decoration, ensuring that one is a mirror image of the other (pages 71 and 138). When dry, place in position on the smallest cake, securing with royal icing and supporting until dry and set.

8 Attach ribbon to the edges of the cake drums. Attach the lace in position over the top of the extension work. Assemble the cakes using separators or pillars.

BRUSH EMBROIDERY

This very attractive direct piping technique produces a thick, padded effect. The outlines of the design are piped with soft peak royal icing, which is then spread into the centre of the outline by brushing with a damp paintbrush.

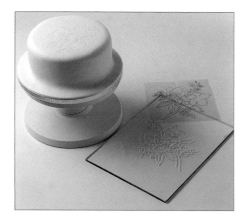

1 Trace the design (page 136) on to greaseproof paper. Turn the paper over and place underneath a sheet of glass or clear perspex. Hold in position with masking tape. Using royal icing and a no. 1 tube (tip), pipe the complete outline on to the glass or perspex. Leave to dry.

2 Transfer the design on to soft sugarpaste or marzipan by pressing the hardened piped design into it. Press firmly, then lift the sheet of glass or perspex away.

3 Start the design by piping an outline with soft peak royal icing. The size of the tube (tip) used will depend upon the size of the design being created; a no. 1 or no. 2 tube is most often used, but you can use a bag with no tube at all, cutting the tip of the bag to the required size.

4 Using a damp brush (usually a no. 2 or no. 3 round paintbrush), touch the surface of the sugar and stroke downwards towards the centre of the shape outlined.

5 Large surface areas can be covered easily and quickly using a flat brush.

6 To create texture, particularly veining in leaves, use a finer brush.

7 Extra depth can be created by piping in the central veins of leaves. This must be done while the leaf is still soft. Extra curl on petals can be created by piping a further layer of royal icing and smoothing down with the flat brush after the first

layer is dry. Stems, buds and flower centres can be piped directly with firm peak royal icing.

8 White brush embroidery on a coloured background can be very effective, providing a soft, padded finish. (Rose template on page 138.)

9 Coloured royal icing gives a much brighter, bolder effect. (Fish template on page 140.)

10 A different, blended effect is created by piping a design in white royal icing and using liquid colours dissolved in water to brush the design outlines. (Butterfly template on page 131.)

11 Once dry, brush embroidery can be finished off with coloured dusts and fine painted lines, achieving varying depths of colour. (Oak leaf template on page 139.)

Piped Flowers

Piped flowers make a pretty addition to any cake, large or small, and are totally edible. Use petal piping tubes (both left- and right-handed tubes are available) and stiff royal icing. If available, add a few drops of acetic acid to the royal icing; this will make the icing stronger ('short'), and the petals will 'break away' more easily when piped. Most piped flowers are made on a flower nail, with small squares of greaseproof or waxed paper stuck to the nail with a little royal icing.

Daisy

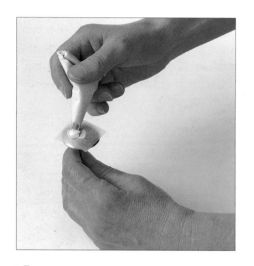

1 Use a no. 57 tube (tip). Lay the thick end of the tube on the centre of the flower nail. Lift the thin end of the tube up slightly (approximately 20°), and pipe the first petal using an upwards and downwards movement with the tube touching the surface of the paper. At the same time, turn the flower nail in an anti-clockwise direction (for right-handed piping) or clockwise direction (for left-handed piping).

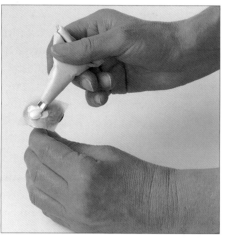

2 Tuck the tube underneath the first petal and repeat the action.

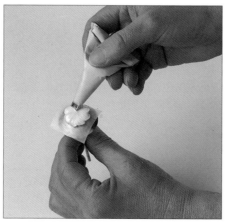

3 Continue this process until you have completed six petals. When piping the final petal, lift the icing up over the first petal.

4 Make the centre, piping a series of small yellow dots with a no. 1 tube.

5 The flower can be removed from the nail, on its square of paper, while still soft.

Daffodil

The outside petals are formed in the same way as for the daisy (left). Brush in a centre vein on each petal using a damp, pointed no. 2 brush, drawing the brush towards the tip of the petal. The trumpet is piped with the tube held vertically and, when dry, may be painted as shown.

Pansy

Pipe two small petals as described for the daisy (left), one overlapping the other. Pipe a further two petals, one on either side of the first two. The final petal is piped in a semi-circular motion from the centre, turning the tube outwards, and then returning it to

the centre. Paint the features on with a fine brush, and pipe in the centre stamen with royal icing.

Chrysanthemum

Pipe a ring of small petals as described for the daisy (left) around the outside edge of the nail. Pipe a further ring of petals inside the first, finally adding a few petals to fill up the centre. When set, dust with a little powder colour.

Rose

A specially designed rose nail or 'cone' is available. This has a non-stick surface that can be piped on to directly without the need for grease-proof or waxed paper.

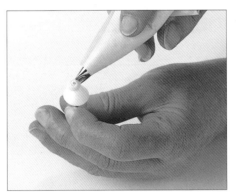

1 Hold the piping bag so that the pointed end of the tube is at the top, over the centre of the rose cone. Pipe a bud by squeezing the icing out to stick to the cone, and

then turning the nail 360° in an anti-clockwise (right-handed piping) or clockwise (left-handed piping) direction. Finish with a downwards action to break the icing off.

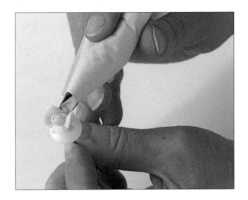

2 Pipe the first row of three petals, this time positioning the narrow point of the tube out slightly, and using an upwards and then a downwards motion to create each petal, turning the cone at the same time.

3 Add the final row of five petals, using the same method as before. Leave to dry on the cone.

4 When set, remove the rose carefully from the cone and fill the back with royal icing piped with a no. 1 tube. Leave to dry, then pipe on a calyx with a no. 1 tube and green royal icing. Leave to dry.

LACE

This is a very delicate decoration which can be used on many types of cake, large or small, royal iced or sugarpasted. You will need to use strong royal icing (made using pure albumen, page 50) for this technique.

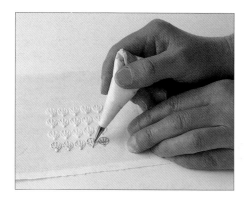

1 Trace your chosen pattern (page 136) on to paper. Place waxed paper over the top and pipe the outlines carefully with a no. 0 tube (tip), ensuring that the lines touch where designed, giving strength to the lace. Take care not to pipe one line through another as this will weaken the lace structure.

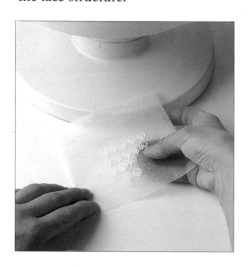

2 When dry, carefully lift the lace by folding back the waxed paper and sliding the lace on to your thumb.

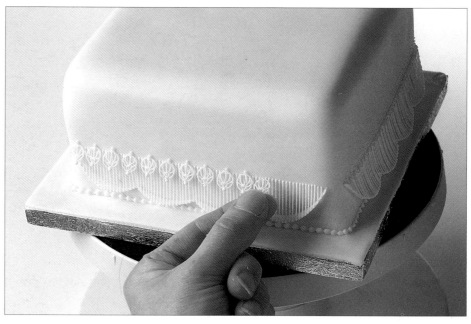

3 Attach to the surface of the cake with a little dot of royal icing, piped on to the edge of the piece of lace.

TULLE

This is a good way of making a fine, delicate, yet strong, decoration. Choose a good, strong nylon tulle.

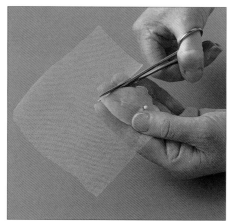

1 Trace the patterns (page 136) on to greaseproof paper. Pin the pattern pieces to tulle and cut out the shapes.

2 Cut pieces of thin card, slightly larger than the tulle pieces, and curl gently over a knife blade. Cut waxed

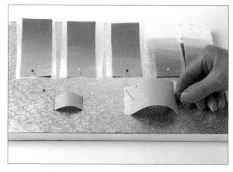

paper the same size and lay over the card. Pin these to a cake drum, securing the sheets of paper and the shapes together.

3 Place the tulle shapes in position on the card and hold flat with your fingertips. Pipe the outline of the tulle with royal icing and a no. 0 tube. Release the card. Pipe in centre veins and leave to dry.

EXPERT ADVICE

Colour the icing as required *before* 'letting down', so the icing does not become too runny.

areas. Use firm peak icing for this, 'let down' with water added a drop at a time until you reach the consistency of double cream. To test the consistency, draw a line across the surface of the icing with a knife; the mark should disappear by the count of 10. Place the icing in a bag without a tube (tip).

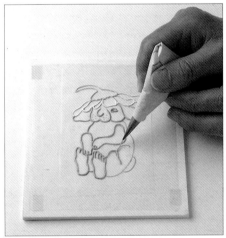

4 Remove the pins from the card. Carefully peel the tulle away from the waxed paper using a fine palette knife or feeler gauge (see Expert Advice). Assemble using firm royal icing in the centre of the flower.

RUNOUTS

This is a very versatile technique using royal icing made with pure albumen (page 50). Drying under a hot lamp (an anglepoise lamp is ideal) is important to produce a good gloss.

2 Fit a second bag with a no. 1 or no. 0 tube and fill with firm icing. Trace the pattern (page 140) on to greaseproof paper. Mark the areas to be filled in the correct order, starting with those furthest away in perspective and finishing with the areas that are closest. Attach the pattern to a piece of stiff board. Lay a sheet of waxed paper, slightly larger than the pattern, over the top and secure with sticky tape or dots of royal icing. Pipe the outlines of the pattern with the firm icing.

EXPERT ADVICE

A feeler gauge is more commonly found in the hand of a car mechanic than a cake decorator! Sold in sets in car maintenance shops, they are used to test the spark plugs in a car's engine! Each set contains numerous different-sized tools similar to fine palette knives – ideal for many cake-decorating purposes.

1 Fill a piping bag with royal icing with which to flood the outlined

3 Cut a small hole, the size of a no. 1 tube, in the bag with the soft icing and begin to 'flood'. Start with the areas marked with a '1', holding the point of the bag close to the outline. Move the bag slowly backwards and forwards, using a little pressure to ease the sugar out, as if you were colouring in a shape with a pencil. As you complete the 'flooding' of this first area, stop the pressure on the bag and remove, from the side of the area and over the piped outline. This ensures that you do not get a mark in the smooth sugar. Place under a hot lamp to allow the sugar to crust only on the top surface.

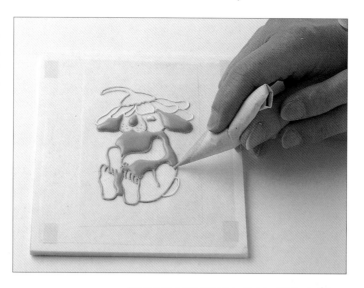

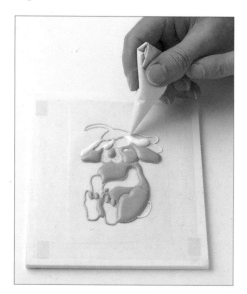

4 Repeat the process for the areas marked with a '2'.

5 Repeat again for the areas marked with a '3'. The pattern

should now be completed. Small pictures like these are called motifs.

6 Place the motif under a hot lamp for a final time to crust the last areas of soft sugar. Do not leave the

EXPERT ADVICE

If you are unsure how long to leave the sugar under the lamp, pipe small bulbs of soft icing on the spare area of paper around the motif. You can squash these to test how the crusting process is progressing.

motif under the lamp for any longer than the crusting process as the sugar and the now-damp paper will dry at different rates and may warp. Place the motif in a dry, warm position until completely set and firm.

7 Apply features by painting with either neat liquid food colouring, or with other types of food colouring mixed with alcohol. Always ensure that the brush holds very little liquid (too much will dissolve the surface of the runout).

8 Textured features can be applied with soft royal icing on a brush.

9 Remove the motif from the paper by peeling in a downwards motion over the edge of a hard surface, e.g. a thick board or the edge of a table.

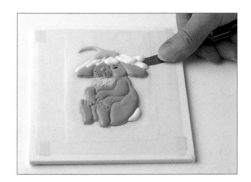

10 Alternatively, separate the motif from the waxed paper by sliding a feeler gauge (see page 71) or fine, flexible palette knife carefully between the two.

11 To fix the motif in its final position, pipe soft royal icing on to the back of the runout. Carefully place the runout in position. *Do not press hard*, as runouts break very easily. (See Easter Bunny Cake, page 80.)

PIPING RUNOUTS DIRECTLY ON TO SUGAR SURFACES

For the confident sugarcrafter, this is a quick way of putting patterns and designs on to cakes.

1 Trace the chosen design (page 133) on to greaseproof paper. Turn the paper over and retrace the reversed pattern so that it is visible. Place a sheet of glass or clear perspex over the reversed design and pipe the outline with a no. 1 tube (tip) and firm royal icing. Leave to dry well.

2 Coat the cake with sugarpaste or marzipan and allow to crust for 5 minutes (to stop the design stick-

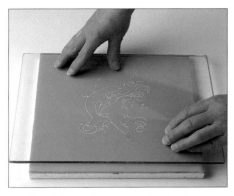

ing). Use the piped design to emboss the surface.

3 With a no. 1 tube and firm royal icing, pipe over the embossed lines.

4 Flood in the areas of the design with soft sugar, as described on page 72. Pipe on details.

Pastillage

'Pastillage' is a French word which has been anglicized to mean a sugar paste mixed with gums to produce a very hard sugar when dry. The finest pastillage is made with royal icing and gum tragacanth. It can be rolled out to quite a fine degree, cut, shaped, curved and moulded to produce a variety of decorations, from tiny wedding bells for decorating wedding cakes to the 'Grand Pièce' centrepieces found on buffet tables. Pastillage work needs careful planning as the paste dries very quickly. All the pattern templates must be ready before you roll out the paste.

Easier to make and handle is gum paste which is a mixture of icing (confectioners') sugar and gelatine solution. This tends to roll out thicker than pastillage but can still be cut, shaped, curved and moulded.

Pastillage

1 teaspoon gum tragacanth
175g (6oz) royal icing (any recipe, page 50)
75g (3oz / ½ cup) icing (confectioners') sugar

1 Mix the gum into the royal icing and leave to mature in a bowl covered with a clean, damp cloth for about 30 minutes.

2 Incorporate the icing sugar by mixing it in either by hand or in a heavy-duty machine with a beater. Immediately wrap in a polythene bag until required for use.

Gum Paste

2 teaspoons powdered gelatine
100ml (4fl oz / ½ cup) cold water
450g (1lb / 3 cups) icing (confectioners') sugar
3 tablespoons cornflour

1 Make the gelatine solution first by mixing the powdered gelatine with the cold water in a saucepan. Leave the mixture to 'sponge' for about 10 minutes, then heat gently, stirring continuously, until it becomes clear.

2 Prepare the sugar by mixing with the cornflour in the bowl of a heavy-duty machine (or large mixing bowl if mixing by hand). Measure out 60ml (2¼ fl oz) gelatine solution (not the full amount you have made) and add to the dry ingredients. Mix together until completely incorporated. Adjust the consistency by adding either more icing sugar or more gelatine solution. Wrap carefully in a polythene bag until required.

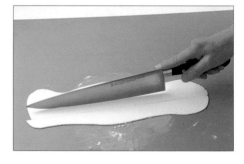

HANDLING PASTILLAGE

1 Ensure you have all your patterns and templates ready for use. (Patterns for the turtle dove design are on page 133.) Roll out the paste to the thickness required on a non-stick board lightly dusted with cornflour. Straight lines should be cut with a long-bladed knife which is not dragged but *rocked* from tip to handle to make the cut.

2 Curves can be cut into the paste with the tip of a sharp pointed knife or with a small cutting wheel. (Alternatively, pastillage can be cut

similar. Do not use glass paper or sandpaper – it is too coarse, can shed glass or sand into your work, and can discolour the sugar.

6 Smooth away any excess royal icing with a damp paintbrush.

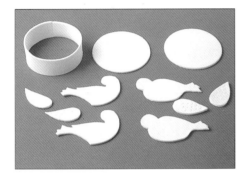

with cutters; dust the edges of your cutters with a little cornflour if your paste is soft, to prevent sticking.)

3 When all the pieces have been cut (including spare pieces in case of breakage), add any embossed features, and leave them to dry on a porous surface, i.e. thick card or a wooden board. The drying time will vary, so cut a few squares of paste from the same roll as the pattern pieces to test. When the pieces are nearly dry, turn them over to dry the underside.

4 Smooth away any rough edges with an emery board or something

5 When the pastillage is dry, paint the pieces as required (see page 76). Assemble the pieces with royal icing, piped as unobtrusively as possible.

7 Leave the assembly to dry completely, supporting the pieces if necessary.

8 Complete the pastillage decoration with any additional painting, and attach ribbons with a little royal icing.

MOULDING PASTILLAGE

Pastillage can be used effectively with moulds, producing a hard surface which is excellent for many painting and colouring techniques.

1 Small moulds can be filled completely to produce solid shapes. Polish the mould first with a soft, dry cloth, then dust lightly with cornflour. (Cornflour wrapped in a little muslin square and tied with a ribbon is an easy way of dispensing a fine dust.) Mould the paste into a smooth ball and press into the mould. Lift the shape out to check it is not sticking and that it has picked up the pattern, then replace in the mould and trim away any excess paste. Turn out on to a porous surface to dry.

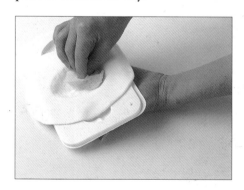

2 For larger moulds, roll out the paste into a sheet slightly larger than the mould. Polish the mould as in step 1, then lay the sheet of pastillage over the prepared mould. Gently press the sheet down into the mould with your fingertips or,

ideally, with a piece of sponge dipped in cornflour. Ensure that the paste is not sticking, trim away any excess, and leave in the mould to dry firm.

3 When the paste is dry, tip the moulded shape out and prepare for the next stage by smoothing the edges to a clean finish (see Handling Pastillage, step 4).

PAINTING PASTILLAGE

1 Pastillage pieces can be painted with liquid colours or with paste or powder colours mixed with clear alcohol (gin or vodka), or with food-grade felt-tipped pens. Pastillage pieces are removed from cakes before cutting so they can also be painted with non-edible gold and silver if required.

2 A selection of dusts can be applied with a flat brush, building up the colour as you wish.

3 A delicate effect for these bells is created by brushing very lightly with a lustre dust, gradually fading the application to the top of the bell.

4 This teddy (below) has been sponged with a mixture of paste colour and alcohol. Carefully done, this gives good coverage of colour yet a flecked effect to represent fur.

Opposite: Mask Cake (page 78)

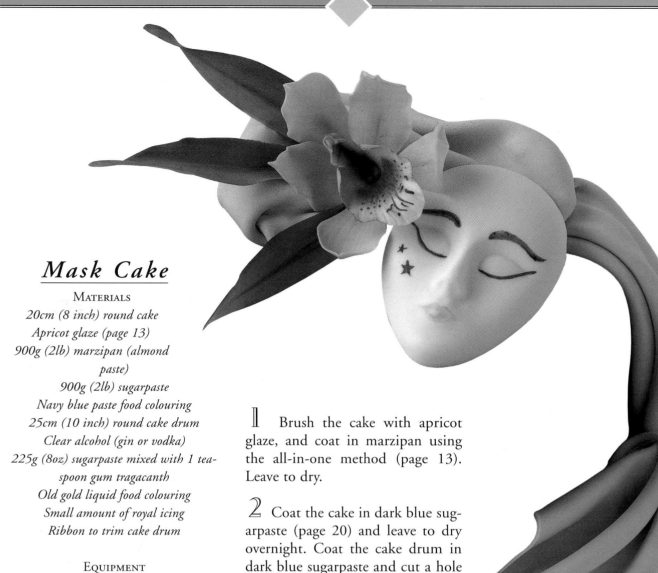

Mask Cake

MATERIALS
20cm (8 inch) round cake
Apricot glaze (page 13)
900g (2lb) marzipan (almond
paste)
900g (2lb) sugarpaste
Navy blue paste food colouring
25cm (10 inch) round cake drum
Clear alcohol (gin or vodka)
225g (8oz) sugarpaste mixed with 1 teaspoon gum tragacanth
Old gold liquid food colouring
Small amount of royal icing
Ribbon to trim cake drum

EQUIPMENT
Icing polishers
Piece of sponge
Dowel rods
Star cutter

DECORATIONS
Pastillage mask (page 76)
Sugar orchid (page 100)
Long leaves (page 103)

1 Brush the cake with apricot glaze, and coat in marzipan using the all-in-one method (page 13). Leave to dry.

2 Coat the cake in dark blue sugarpaste (page 20) and leave to dry overnight. Coat the cake drum in dark blue sugarpaste and cut a hole slightly off centre in which to place the cake (page 22). Position the cake and neaten the join at the bottom of the cake.

3 Mix some navy blue paste colouring with alcohol, and lightly sponge all the blue sugarpaste to deepen and fleck the colour (page 25). Leave to dry.

4 Colour the strengthened sugarpaste with old gold liquid colouring, roll out and cut long rectangles. Using the techniques for drapes on page 36, carefully drape the paste on to the cake using as many pieces as you need. Glue into position with a little cool boiled water applied to the cake with a brush, making sure you cover any pinched pleats in the paste. Cut some stars from leftover gold sugarpaste, and attach to the cake side with cool boiled water.

5 Position the mask on the cake with a little royal icing. Push the orchid and leaves into the folds of the gold sugarpaste. Attach a ribbon to the edge of the cake drum to complete.

ROYAL ICING COLLARS

Collars make an attractive frame for a cake. They can enhance a design and give the cake greater importance, making it look more impressive. Collars also make a cake appear larger than it really is. When designing a cake with a collar, remember to measure the overall finished size of cake and collar, and ensure that the cake drum is larger than this measurement.

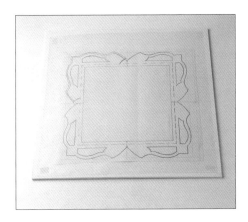

1 Trace the required collar design (page 140) and place underneath a sheet of waxed paper. Attach to a flat board with small pieces of sticky tape or dots of royal icing.

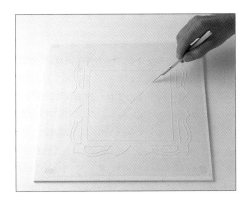

2 Pipe the outlines with a no. 1 or no. 0 tube (tip) and firm royal icing. Score the waxed paper with a scalpel, making a cross in the centre of the paper and a slit in the paper between each corner of the collar and the glued corner of the paper. This will stop the runout warping whilst drying, as the sugar and the damp waxed paper will dry at different speeds.

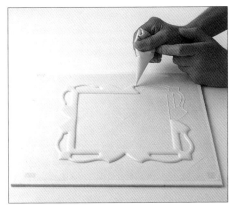

3 Soften the royal icing, adding a drop of water at a time, until the icing is the consistency of single cream. Draw the blade of a knife across the surface of the icing; the line should disappear by the count of five. Place the icing in a large greaseproof paper bag without a tube. Cut a no. 2 hole in the bag and squeeze the icing into a second large greaseproof bag. This should remove many of the air bubbles created during the mixing. Be careful not to trap further air bubbles during this process. To ensure that this doesn't happen, make sure that the stream of icing flows along the inner edge of the piping bag (it's a bit like pouring a pint of beer). Cut a no. 2 hole in the new bag and start flooding the collar. Flood in small areas at a time, working around the area as if working around a clock face, i.e. start at 12, then move to 11, then 1, 10, 2 and so on.

4 Place the collar under a hot lamp to crust the surface of the sugar. Remove the collar from under the lamp and leave in a warm, dry position until completely firm and hard. To check how the icing is progressing, pipe some bulbs of icing on spare areas of waxed paper. These can be squashed to test crusting and drying speeds.

5 When the collar is dry, release it from the waxed paper by easing a fine palette knife or feeler gauge (see page 71) between the two, gently working your way around.

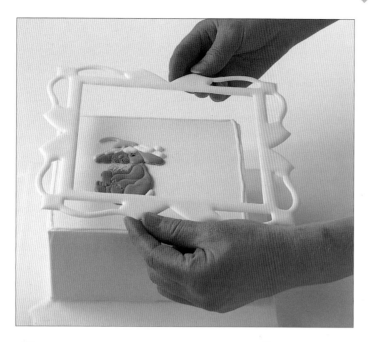

6 Pipe softened royal icing along the top edges of the cake and carefully lift the collar into position. *Do not press.* Leave to dry.

7 To complete the effect, pipe 3-2-1 linework in firm royal icing (page 57).

Easter Bunny Cake

MATERIALS
15cm (6 inch) square cake
Apricot glaze (page 13)
900g (2lb) marzipan (almond paste)
23cm (9 inch) square cake drum
Royal icing made with albumen substitute
(page 50)
Yellow and green paste food colourings
Royal icing made with pure albumen
(page 50)
Ribbon to trim cake drum

EQUIPMENT
Icing ruler
Side scraper
Piping bags
Nos. 0, 1, 2 and 3 piping tubes (tips)

1 Brush the cake with apricot glaze, and coat in marzipan using the top and sides method (page 14).

2 Place the cake on the cake drum, and coat in three layers of yellow royal icing made with albumen substitute, leaving each coat to dry before applying the next (page 51). Coat the cake drum around the cake (page 53). Leave to dry.

3 Make the bunny motif (page 71). Using the templates on page 140, make the top collar and corner collars for the base of the cake (page 79).

4 Attach the bunny motif in position with soft royal icing, then attach the top and bottom collars.

5 Pipe 3-2-1 linework (page 57) in yellow royal icing around the edges of the collar on the top of the cake.

6 Pipe bulbs with a no. 2 tube around the base of the cake above the corner collars.

7 Use tube embroidery techniques (page 63) to pipe grass and flowers around the bunny and on the sides of the cake. Pipe an inscription with a no. 1 tube (page 82). Attach a ribbon to the edge of the cake drum.

LETTERING

This method of personalizing cakes and sending messages to the recipient should always be legible. Match the style of lettering not only to the cake design, but to the recipient of the cake. For example, small children can more easily read lettering in upper and lower case letters. Templates for lettering and numerals are provided on pages 141–142.

1 The lettering shown here is piped with a no. 1 tube (tip). Pipe the lettering in a colour to match the colour of the cake. Mistakes can be easily removed without leaving marks. Coloured overpiping can then be added. Having practised simple lettering, flounces and embellishments can be added if required.

2 Different techniques in piping can further style the lettering using lines, dots and loops.

3 Inscriptions such as 'Happy Anniversary' are often added to cakes. Practise on waxed paper and hold this in position over the cake to judge where you will pipe the final design. Practise to develop your own personal style.

4 Runout lettering gives a bolder effect. Use a runout first letter only, if you wish, when writing in straight lines. Runout complete names can be arranged more easily in curves (e.g. Caron). Glue into position with a little soft royal icing when you have achieved the desired arrangement.

5 Numerals can be treated in many ways, either piped directly on to the cake or in runout form.

6 Illuminated letters can be used where there is no other decoration, or when the lettering is a feature of the decoration.

SUGAR FLOWERS

Moulding sugar flowers is an absorbing aspect of sugarcraft. Besides being used to decorate cakes, sugar flowers can be made into attractive arrangements in their own right, as table centrepieces, bouquets or gifts. There are many basic methods for making flowers, starting with 'pulled' flowers, such as freesias, primroses and jasmine. Different techniques are used to make 'cutter' flowers, which include orchids, roses and carnations. Combined with sugar foliage and ribbon loops, etc., they all look most attractive arranged in sprays, bouquets or posies, or in natural settings.

MAKING AND USING FLOWER PASTE

The paste required to make fine flowers and foliage is available commercially under a variety of names (e.g. flower paste and petal paste), but you can make your own if necessary.

Flower Paste

You will need a heavy-duty mixing machine with a beater attachment for this recipe to produce a good result. This flower paste cannot be made by hand, using a hand-held electric mixer or in a food processor.

400g (14oz) icing (confectioners') sugar
50g (2oz/ ½ cup) cornflour
3 teaspoons gum tragacanth or 2 teaspoons gum tragacanth and 2 teaspoons carboxy-methyl-cellulose (CMC)
5 teaspoons cold water
2 teaspoons powdered gelatine
3 teaspoons white vegetable fat (shortening)
2 teaspoons liquid glucose
1 large egg white, strained

1 Sift the sugar, cornflour and gum tragacanth together into the bowl from your machine, and warm. This can be done in a variety of ways: a metal or glass bowl can be placed in a low-heat oven; a plastic bowl can be put in the microwave on a warm setting. Alternatively, place the bowl over a pan of hot water. In all cases, cover the bowl with a clean tea-towel to stop the surface of the dry ingredients crusting, and warm the beater from the machine as well. Be careful not to make the ingredients too hot. They should be just warm to the touch.

2 Measure the water into a cup or small container and add the gelatine. Allow to stand for a few minutes to 'sponge', i.e. for the gelatine crystals to absorb the water.

3 Warm the gelatine mixture by standing the cup in hot water until the mixture is runny and clear.

4 Add the white fat and liquid glucose to the gelatine mixture and stir until the fat has melted.

EXPERT ADVICE

Liquid glucose is difficult to measure because it is extremely sticky. Use a wet spoon or the spoon the fat was measured with. Remember to use level spoon measures.

5 Add the gelatine mixture and the egg white to the warmed, dry ingredients, and mix together on a slow speed until the ingredients are incorporated together.

6 Turn the mixer to full speed and beat until the paste becomes white and stringy. If you hear the machine motor straining, turn the speed down a little.

7 Remove the paste from the bowl and immediately wrap in a polythene bag. Place in a small, plastic, lidded container, and place in the refrigerator to mature for 24 hours before use. For ease of use, wrap small pieces of paste individually before chilling.

HANDLING FLOWER PASTE

1 When you take the paste from the refrigerator it will be very hard. This is an indication that the recipe has worked successfully. Cut off a small amount of paste and knead well. The paste becomes workable with the warmth of your hands and the friction caused whilst kneading it. Alternatively, warm in the microwave on defrost for about 30 seconds, then knead with fingertips.

2 The paste should be quite elastic and will 'snap' when you pull it apart. The paste dries out quickly, so keep it covered, either in a polythene bag or a small pot.

MAKING THE PASTE WORK FOR YOU

You may have to add extra amounts of some of the ingredients so that the paste performs to your liking.

CORNFLOUR Add extra if the paste is soft and too elastic. This may be due to the type of paste used, too much liquid added at the mixing stage, kneading with very hot hands, or colouring the paste with liquid or paste colouring.

EGG WHITE Add extra if the paste is too dry. This may be due to there not being enough liquid in the mix, or to the paste being old.

WHITE FAT Add extra if the paste is very firm. This may be due to the type of paste used, the paste starting to dry out, or colouring the paste with a powder colouring. If the paste is feeling sticky (due to the addition of too much extra egg white), add more white fat to balance the ingredients.

GUM TRAGACANTH Add extra if the paste is soft and doesn't 'snap'. This may be due to the type of paste used, or to adding too little or insufficiently warm gum.

USING GLUE

Edible glue is frequently used when making sugar flowers. There is a wide choice for you to select from. We don't think any one has any advantage over the others.

FRESH EGG WHITE This is simple to use but we do not recommend it for flowers that are to be used on a cake due to the slight risk of salmonella being present.

RECONSTITUTED ALBUMEN POWDER Place 5 teaspoons cool boiled water in a small jar. Add 1 teaspoon pure albumen, pop the lid on, shake well and leave overnight.

GUM ARABIC SOLUTION Place 10 teaspoons orange flower water in a small jar. Add 2 teaspoons gum arabic powder, pop the lid on, shake well and leave overnight to soak. This produces a jelly.

PREPARING WIRES

Wires are graded in SWG or 'gauge'. The higher the number, the finer the wire. Wires for sugar flowers are available in many different coloured paper wraps. Remove a small bundle of wires from the packet and cut into four smaller lengths, using heavy-duty scissors or wire cutters. Providing the paste on your flower

is still soft and not dry you should be able to use your wire straight. However, if your paste starts to dry prematurely you may need to make a small hook in the end of the wire to bed it into the paste. You may also need to use hooked wires for larger flowers as this gives extra strength and support to the base of the flower. An easy way to form a hook in a wire is to turn the end over using a small pair of pointed tweezers.

STEAMING

Steaming sets the powder colour into the paste and gives a slight natural sheen to the flowers. By repeating the steaming process you can build up a stronger gloss. When steaming, you are actually cooking the outer layer of sugar. To steam flowers safely, boil a kettle until you get a full jet of steam from the spout. Hold the flower or leaf in the jet of steam for a second or two. (You will need to hold the switch on for automatic kettles.) Leave to dry for a few minutes. Steaming is also ideal for refreshing sprays of flowers which have become dusty or dull. Just move the spray around in the jet of steam for 5 seconds or so, or until all the flowers shine. Leave the spray to dry.

Pulled Flowers

Also known as filler flowers, this is a good place to start when learning to use flower paste.

Jasmine

1 Take a small piece of white paste and roll it into a ball (above left). Model to a teardrop shape (above right).

2 Dip the pointed end of a dowel into white fat (shortening) and rub into the wood. This will stop the paste sticking to the dowel. Push the pointed end of the dowel into the rounded end of the teardrop.

3 Either cut five equal-sized slits with a scalpel into the large end of the teardrop only before removing it from the dowel (right), or remove the teardrop from the dowel and cut with fine pointed scissors (far right).

4 Open up the petals by pushing your finger into the centre.

5 Taking each petal in turn, shape by first pinching the cut edges

inwards and then squashing flat with your thumb on the top and your index finger on the underside. Finish this action with a gentle flick upwards with your thumb.

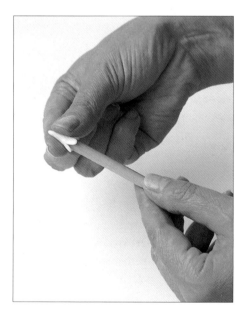

6 Place the pointed end of the dowel back into the centre of the flower and ease the petals upwards gently to produce a more natural shape.

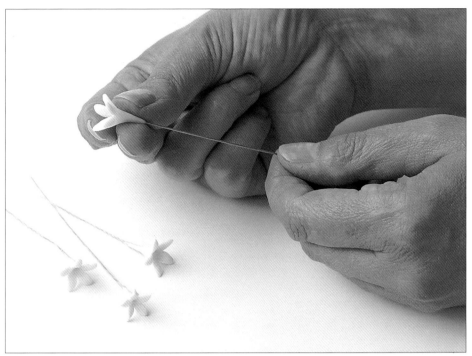

7 Thread a short length of 28- or 30-gauge green wire through the throat of the flower until the tip of the wire sits in the soft paste at the back of the flower. Gently roll this paste on to the wire to secure. Allow the flowers to dry and harden overnight before dusting to the required finish, using a soft flat brush. See Expert Advice for colour ideas.

8 Tape jasmine flowers and buds (page 105) together in natural sprays using ½-width green florists' tape.

EXPERT ADVICE

There are many types of jasmine, making it an ideal flower for a variety of uses. It is quick and simple to make and is therefore a good 'filler' flower. The winter jasmine is a lovely dark yellow colour; summer jasmine is white with a yellow centre and a touch of pink on the petals. Copying the real flower, if in season, or looking in a good botanical reference book, will help you achieve the most lifelike shapes and colours.

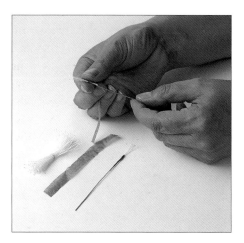

EXPERT ADVICE

A bunch of fresh flowers to copy is a great help when modelling sugar flowers.

Freesia

1 Prepare the wires first. Tape six fine stamens to the tip of each green wire, using ¼-width green florists' tape. Make the assembly as smooth as possible.

2 Take a small piece of paste and roll it into a smooth ball, then model to a teardrop shape. Dip the pointed end of a dowel into white fat (shortening) and rub into the wood. Push the pointed end of the dowel into the large end of the teardrop, smoothing the tail of the teardrop into a slender point. Cut six slits in the large end of the paste, either with a scalpel or scissors (as for Jasmine, page 86).

3 Pinch the cut edges of a petal inwards, and then squash the petal

flat, pinching the outer edge to give a slight point. Repeat for all six petals.

4 Use the dowel to roll the petals thinly, using the edge of a non-stick board as support. Roll the petals first from the centre out to each side.

5 Finish by rolling out towards the edge of the petal to accentuate the pointed lip. Use the shoulder of the dowel point to cup the petal.

6 Place the flower on a throat modelling tool and push three alternate petals up and the other three down. Take two of the petals going upwards and lay the one pointing downwards between them, up over the top. Press firmly to join, and repeat with the rest of the petals. Remove from the modelling tool and moisten the centre of the flower with glue.

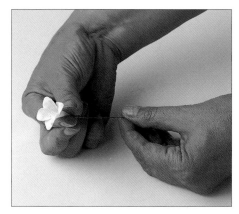

7 Gently feed a prepared wire through the throat of the flower, rolling the base well to bed on to the wire. Finally, shape the throat to the desired finish and shape the tips of the petals into a natural arrangement.

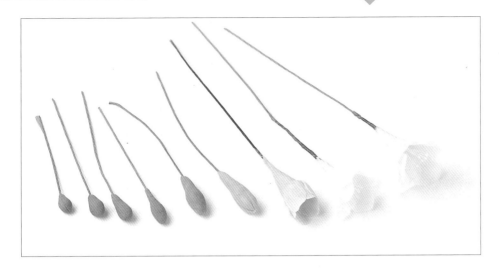

a little egg white on the inside and outside of the throat. This acts as a barrier when brushing on the coloured powder, leaving the throat white. Use a flat brush to dust the petals the required colour, then use a fine brush to add a little yellow dust to the tips of the stamens and inside the throat.

8 Make some more flowers, slightly less open, and some buds. The buds are elongated teardrops, made in green paste. Make the smallest buds first on to straight 28-gauge wires. As you make larger buds, add a little white paste to the green to lighten the colour. The largest buds should be marked across the top with three lines made with a veiner tool or scalpel (page 105).

base of the flower, allowing the two long points to stand proud.

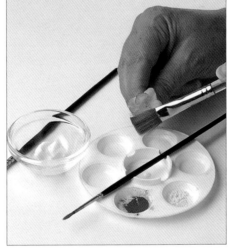

11 Tape the flowers and buds together as shown, then arrange naturally. If you wish to use these flower sprays in a vase, tape in a florists' stub wire (16–18-gauge) to strengthen the stem.

9 The calyx for each flower is a tiny diamond of green paste. Glue the calyx, pick up with the wire, push up and press gently around the

10 Allow the flowers to dry and harden overnight before dusting to the required colour. Freesias have a white throat and coloured petals. If you are new to dusting, rub a little white vegetable fat or paint

Blossom

1 Roll a small piece of paste into a smooth ball, then model into a teardrop. Dip the pointed end of a dowel rod into white fat (shortening) and rub into the wood. Push the point of the dowel into the wide end of the teardrop, and cut five petals with a scalpel or scissors (as for Jasmine, page 86). Roll each petal from side to side with the dowel on the edge of a non-stick board.

2 Remove the flower from the dowel and arrange the petals in a natural shape. Push on to a 28-gauge wire. Push two or three short stamens, dipped in glue, into the throat of the flower, using tweezers. Make as many flowers as required and allow to dry overnight.

3 Dust the edges of the petals and the throats with colour, using a soft, flat brush.

4 Make some buds (page 105) and tape with the blossoms into a spray.

EXPERT ADVICE

Blossoms and their buds are useful 'filler' flowers, which can be used individually or in sprays to fill gaps in large arrangements. Make more than you need, in white paste, and store the 'spares' in a box until needed. Dust the blossoms the required colour before you use them.

EXPERT ADVICE

These simple flowers are very popular, and look very pretty tied in a bunch with ribbon. Trim the wires to the same length, tie with a ribbon and bow, and place directly on the cake. If possible, choose a ribbon to match the ribbon used to trim the cake board.

Violet

1 Colour the paste first with violet colouring. Take a small ball of paste, roll smooth and model into a teardrop. Dip the pointed end of a dowel rod into white fat (shortening) and rub into the wood. Push the pointed end of the dowel into the large end of the teardrop, then remove and, using scissors, cut two small (at the top), two medium (one each side), and one large petal (at the bottom) in the opened end of the teardrop.

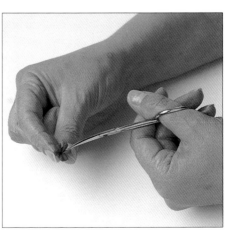

2 Pinch and flatten each petal, easing the top pair and the bottom one backwards slightly, and tweaking the two side petals inwards and upwards. Allow the flowers to dry and harden overnight.

3 Dust the centre of the flower with yellow, and then paint lines with a fine brush and black colouring mixed with alcohol.

4 Arrange the flowers, and buds if required (page 105), in a spray, and tie with a ribbon, if wished.

Primrose

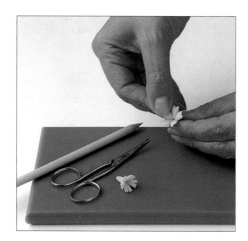

1 Start a primrose with yellow flower paste. Shape and cut as for blossom (step 1, page 90). With a scalpel or scissors, make a shorter cut halfway between each of the five cuts already made. Pinch each petal lightly, then flatten.

2 Roll the petals with the dowel on the edge of a non-stick board, ensuring that each petal has a heart shape. Push the flower on to a 28-gauge wire and roll the back to secure.

3 Make the calyx for the primrose with a very small ball of green paste, rolled into a teardrop and then pushed on to the dowel. Remove from the dowel, paint a little glue

into the hole and push on to the wire, fitting it over the back of the flower. Pinch five protrusions lengthways in the green paste with cranked tweezers. Allow the flowers to dry and harden overnight. Dust the centres of the flowers with green colour.

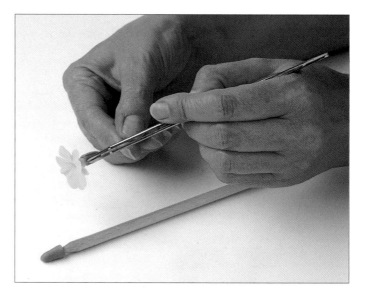

4 Make buds (page 105) and wire into a spray with the flowers. Leaves can be added (page 102).

Honeysuckle

1 Roll a tiny piece of paste (half the size used for jasmine) to a smooth ball, and then model into a long, slender teardrop. Place the wide end on a satay stick or cocktail stick (toothpick) and, with a scalpel or scissors, make the first two cuts, producing one petal consisting of a quarter of the paste. Cut away two

triangles, one from the base of each of these cuts, to finish with a second petal that is thicker but the same width as the first. Cut three slits into this second petal, half the length of the first slits, to produce what looks like a little hand.

2 Using a dowel rod, roll the long, single petal over the top knuckle of your forefinger to flatten and lengthen the petal.

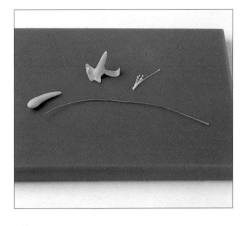

3 Thin the four smaller petals, after pinching and flattening each, with the dowel rod, rolling lightly across them. Turn the flower over and curl the petals back, rolling inwards with a cocktail stick. Push on a 28-gauge wire and smooth the back of the flower, pressing lightly to give a slight curve. Cut six fine stamens, one longer than the other five, trim, dip in egg white or glue and, holding them with tweezers, push them into the throat of the flower. Make buds and push on to curved wires. Allow the flowers to dry and harden overnight before dusting to the required finish.

4 Wire the flowers and buds together in natural sprays, adding leaves as required (page 102).

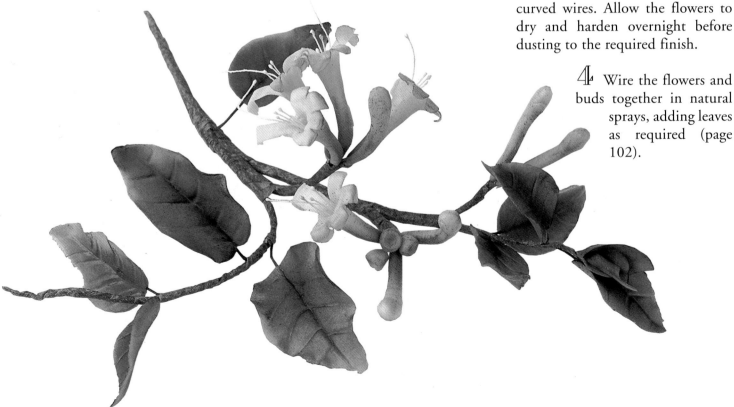

CUTTER FLOWERS

There are hundreds of flower cutters available commercially. Once you have mastered the basic techniques involved in handling the paste for use with cutters, and building the flowers with or without wires, then you are well armed to handle any cutter. Cutter flowers may be made in one whole piece of paste, or from individual petals, or each petal can be wired on a 32- or 33-gauge wire and taped together when all the components are dry.

Stephanotis

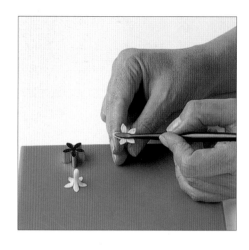

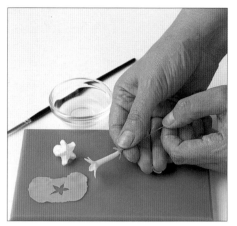

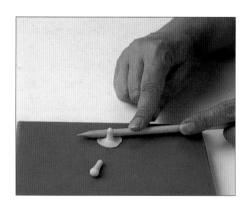

1   This flower is made from one piece of paste. Roll a small piece of paste into a smooth ball, and then into a dumb-bell shape with one end slightly larger than the other. Hold the dumb-bell shape upright and squash the larger end down on to a non-stick board to flatten. Using thumb and forefinger, flatten this area until it is large enough to roll into a circle with a dowel.

2   Drop a stephanotis cutter over the top of the dumb-bell shape, and cut out the shape from the flattened circle. Smooth the edges on the back

of each petal with a small ball-shaped modelling tool. Turn the flower over and mark or thin the centre of each petal with a dresden tool, cocktail stick (toothpick) or the back of a small pointed knife. You may need to do this over the knuckle of your forefinger. Push the flower on to a 26-gauge wire, ensuring the dumb-bell shape is retained and, if possible, elongated.

3   Cut a very small calyx from green paste with a calyx cutter. Add a touch of glue and feed up the wire on to the base of the flower.

4   Arrange the flowers, with buds if desired (page 105), into small sprays. These flowers can be used in mixed flower sprays, wired in individually.

Carnation

1 Prepare a 24-gauge wire by bending a hook in one end. Take a tiny piece of paste and wrap it around the hook. Leave to dry. Roll out some paste quite thinly and place on a non-stick board dusted with a little cornflour. Cut the paste with a carnation cutter. Frill the cut edges of the paste with a cocktail stick (toothpick).

2 Paint a little glue on the flat central area of the circle, push the wire through the centre point and fold the circle in half around the wire. Paint glue on the right-hand third of the half circle and fold in. Turn the flower over and repeat. Pick the flower up, squeeze the unfrilled paste together quite firmly, and roll on to the wire. Leave to dry.

3 Cut another thin piece of paste with the carnation cutter, and frill as in step 1. Glue the paste in the middle of the circle and fold in half. Glue one side of the semi-circle remaining, and wrap around the centre of the dried flower. Smooth the join down with fingertips or a cocktail stick. Leave to dry.

4 Make the calyx with a small ball of green paste modelled to a teardrop. Place the rounded end on to a dowel and cut five shallow points with a scalpel or scissors. Roll the paste, still on the dowel, on a

textured surface, e.g. a piece of dried corn leaf. Remove the paste from the dowel, paint a little glue in the hole, and feed up the wire, pushing neatly around the base of the flower.

5 With the scissors, make five fine snips into the paste as shown (below). Dust the flowers as desired and arrange into sprays, posies or natural arrangements.

Rose

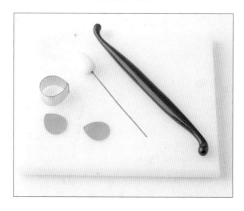

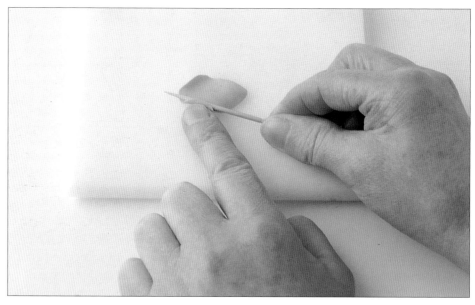

1 Make central cones of paste on hooked 24-gauge wires. The cones should fit inside the petal cutter you have chosen. Leave to dry. Cut one petal and soften the edges with a ball tool. Paint the surface of the petal with glue and wrap it tightly around the cone so that the cone cannot be seen down through the top of the rolled petal. Leave to dry. Cut a second petal, soften the edges, and glue the bottom half. Wrap this around the first petal, opening the top edge slightly.

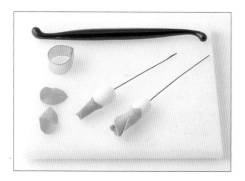

2 Cut two more petals, and add to the rose in the same way as the second petal, this time adding the two petals at the same time, overlapping the edges. Cut three petals, and repeat the process, this time adding all three at the same time. Open up the top edges of the petals and very gently curl them back slightly with your fingertips.

3 The rose will now have grown in size. Select a rose petal cutter one size larger than the one you started with, and cut four or five petals. Soften the edges with a ball tool and cup the centres, then turn the petals over and soften the edges again with the ball tool. Use a cocktail stick (toothpick) to curl back the edges of each petal from the sides of the top edge. Leave to become leathery (about 10 minutes) before gluing the bottom third of each petal, and then adding to the flower.

4 Add further shaping to the petals with your fingertips, then dust the roses with powder colour, and steam (page 85).

5 Make the calyx from green and cream paste, both colours rolled out very thinly. Lay the cream on top of the green and cut out a calyx with a cutter. Cut small snips down the sides of each sepal of the calyx, then soften all edges with a ball tool, working on the green side. Turn the calyx over, cup the centre and glue. Push up the wire and gently press on to the back of the flower. Take a small pea of green paste, glue and push up to the back of the calyx. Smooth neatly into position.

6 Tape the wires with ½-width tape, two or three times, to make the stems more realistic in thickness. Make leaves (page 102) and rosebuds (which start the same way as the flowers but without the open and curled petals added) and wire into a natural arrangement. Roses can be wired individually into mixed flower sprays as well.

Blackberry

The blackberry uses many different modelling techniques. You can include blossom, fruit, buds and leaves in a spray of blackberry, not forgetting a sugar ladybird to add interest.

1   Start by making balls of paste (purple for ripe fruit; green for unripe) approximately three-quarters the size required for the finished berries. Push on to hooked 24-gauge wires. Leave these to dry and harden well.

2   Make tiny balls of paste, coloured as shown, approximately 20 at a time, and glue on to the hardened paste, positioning with tweezers. Use light pressure with fingertips to push into the correct position, flattening the tiny balls slightly.

3   When dry, glaze the berries with neat confectioners' varnish painted on with a brush. Only a thin coat is required. Leave to dry.

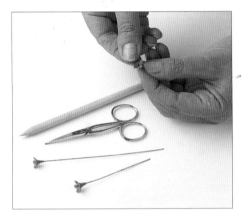

4   To make a blossom, first model a calyx of green paste, following the instructions for the jasmine flower (page 86), but making the calyx much smaller. Wire on to a 26-gauge wire and leave to dry.

5   Cut individual tiny rose petals (five for each blossom). Soften the

edges with a ball tool and cup the centres, then turn the petals over and soften the edges again with the ball tool. Paint glue on the calyx and attach the petals, overlapping each one and tucking the final petal under the first. Paint the centre of the flower lightly with glue, and push a small bundle of cut yellow stamens into the centre, using tweezers. Leave to dry.

6 Buds are made from small round balls of paste on 30-gauge wires. The tiny calyxes are painted on with a fine brush and green colouring.

7 Make leaves of various sizes with rose leaf cutters and veiners (page 102). Wire blossoms, berries, buds and leaves together in a natural arrangement. A sugar ladybird adds interest to the spray: mould a ball of red paste, flatten slightly and leave to dry, then paint with black food colouring. Leave to dry, then fix in position on a blackberry leaf with a little glue.

Orchid

1 This flower will be much easier to make if you have a real one to copy. Start with a large ball of paste modelled into a sausage that is thicker at one end. Push this on to four 32-gauge white wires which have been twisted tightly together and taped with ¼-width white florists' tape. (The twisting of the wire will give strength to this heavy flower.)

Run a scriber down one side of the sausage. Ensure that the top of the sausage remains round and smooth as you squeeze and flatten the sides of the tool-marked area outwards. When you are satisfied with the shape, bend the sausage with the wire inside to give a gentle curve. Pinch a small ball shape into the tip of the sausage, and squeeze the paste neatly around the wire at the other end. Leave to dry.

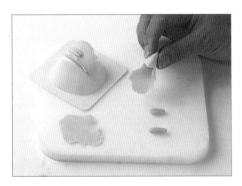

2 This particular orchid is quite fleshy so do not roll out the paste too thinly from now on. Roll out the paste and cut the throat shape with an orchid throat cutter. Vein with a veining tool or soft throat veiner. Soften the furled edges of the throat with a ball tool or flat scriber, and lightly thin the sides of the throat. Place in a throat former to become leathery but not hard. Make the fleshy stamens from a tiny sausage of paste, scored down the middle with a scalpel and flattened when glued into position on the throat. After about 10 minutes, glue the throat to the flower centre, hold for a few moments with your fingertips and then rest back in the throat former until hard.

3 Cut five petals, two with pointed tips and three with rounded edges, using orchid petal cutters. When rolling out the paste, leave a small ridge of thicker paste that will run down the centre of each petal to receive a 32-gauge wire (page 102). Soften the edges of the petals, and vein with a veining tool or veining pad. Carefully insert the 32-gauge

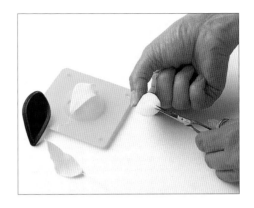

wires, two-thirds the length of each petal. Cup each petal over the pad of your thumb. To further cup the round-edged petals, paint a little glue in the centre of the top edge and pinch the paste together quite firmly. Turn each petal over and cut away the excess paste with scissors. Leave the petals to dry on rounded supports. When dry, dust as required.

4 When the throat assembly is hard, paint and dust as required. Patterns will depend upon the orchid you are making – there are thousands of varieties!

BROOKLANDS COLLEGE LIBRARY
WEYBRIDGE, SURREY KT13 8TT

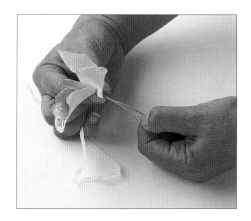

5 Using ¼-width white tape, tape on the two pointed petals (they will look a little like rabbits' ears above the centre of the flower). Add one rounded petal between these two and then the two final petals at the bottom under the throat, allowing the petals to cup naturally around the centre.

6 Tape the flower well, and then arrange it naturally, holding the petals at their base, with tweezers or fingertips.

ORCHID CORSAGE

The corsage requires variegated ivy (page 103), white pulled jasmine flowers and buds (page 86) and two orchids. Tape the orchids together first so that they fit snugly together without the risk of breaking. Tape the leaves into natural sprays, adding the jasmine and buds, and then tape these to the back of the orchids. Ensure that you tape over any cut ends of wires to make a neat presentation. Finally, arrange into the required shape, using tweezers or fingertips.

LEAVES

Once mastered, the basic technique for leaves can be applied to nearly any leaf. Rose leaves are shown here.

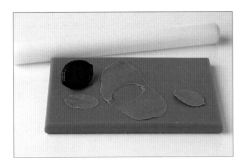

1   Roll out some green flower paste, angling the rolling pin slightly to create a wedge of thicker paste. (Alternatively, use a grooved board or rolling pin, commercially manufactured for this purpose.) Cut out a leaf, positioning the cutter so that the ridge of thicker paste is at the base of the leaf.

2   Soften the edge of the leaf with a dogbone tool on the palm of your hand or a pad of hard foam.

3   Dip a 26- or 28-gauge wire (depending on the size of the leaf) into glue, and then carefully push the wire into the ridge of paste in the leaf. Smooth the join.

4   Vein the leaf in a leaf veiner, then remove the leaf and pinch the back of the centre vein with thumb and forefinger to give greater definition.

5   Colour the leaf with dusts as required; steam (page 85) to give a natural gloss.

6   Tape the leaves together in natural sprays, or use individually in arrangements.

OTHER LEAVES

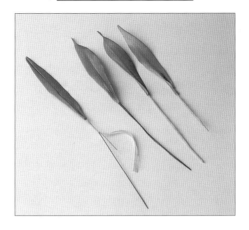

LONG LEAVES Hang long leaves up to dry straight, twisting and curving as required with fingertips. Use a 28-gauge wire inside the leaf and tape on a heavier wire to give strength when the leaf is dry.

HOLLY This is a particularly shiny leaf which will need to be glazed with confectioners' varnish when the leaf has been coloured. Berries are made from small balls of red paste, individually wired and glazed.

SHAMROCK This pretty little leaf should be veined with a veining tool, each leaf of the three in the assembly being treated individually and tweaked to give natural shape.

OTHER LEAF SHAPES (below) Gingko leaves (left) have soft curved stems. Oak leaves can be made in cream paste and dusted with a variety of green and brown dusts. They are shown here wired with twigs

(page 104). The spray on the right shows how rose leaves, cut using a particular brand of rose leaf cutter, and taped around a central stem in pairs, give a very different result from the rose leaf spray on page 102. This is a useful leaf in arrangements.

VARIEGATED LEAVES There are many ways to variegate sugar leaves; the method you choose depends on the effect required. Ivy leaves generally have cream edges and two or three different greens dappled over the centre. Use a fine brush or a small piece of sponge to paint on the colours. Alternatively, paint all the edges of cream-coloured leaves with egg white and leave to dry before dusting the leaves with a variety of green petal dusts; the egg white acts as a barrier, keeping the edges cream-coloured.

TAPE LEAVES

These are useful in an arrangement to protect delicate flowers from touching each other and possibly breaking. They are also useful if you are unable to cut these leaves easily from flower paste.

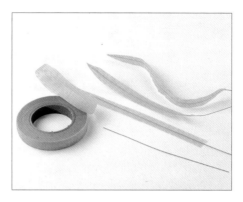

DAFFODIL LEAF Lay a strip of tape flat, sticky side up, and place a 28-gauge wire along half its length. Fold the tape over the end of the wire, and press firmly to join the two lengths of tape together, encasing the wire. Use scissors to trim a point in the top of the tape and to curve the bottom into the wire. Curl, curve and twist as desired.

FERN Make the daffodil type leaf (above) and, while the leaf is still flat, make tiny snips diagonally into the tape on both sides of the wire. Twist the tape around the wire for a very frilled effect. Different effects can be achieved by using two colours of tape.

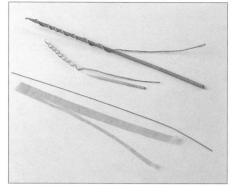

CREEPERS AND TENDRILS Cut a length of ½-width florists' tape and twist it, stretching the tape to release the glue as you do so. Coil the twisted tape around a cocktail stick (toothpick) or satay stick, then gently pull the stick away, leaving the tape coiled as required.

TWIGS

1 Twist ½-width brown tape on to a 24- or 26-gauge wire. After about 2.5cm (1 inch) has been cov-

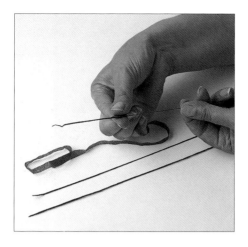

ered, gently pull the wire downwards, almost out of the tape. Continue wrapping tape, leaving an unwired twist of tape at the top. Continue to tape, adding extra wires to create thickness if required, depending on the length of twig needed.

2 Use tweezers or fingertips to bend the taped wire into natural shapes.

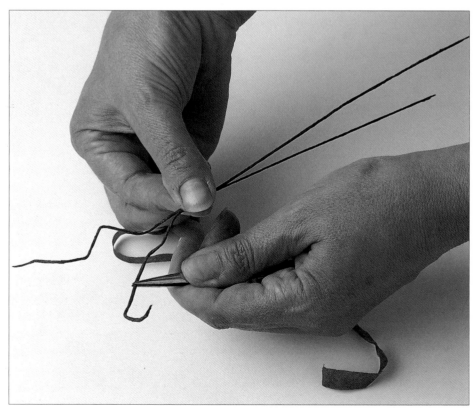

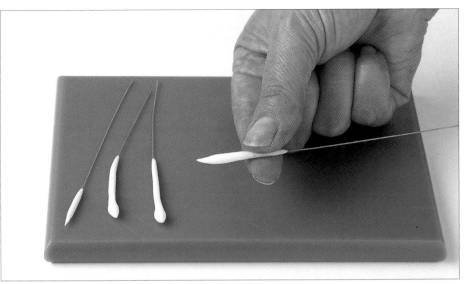

BUDS

1 Four types of buds are shown above; the shape will depend upon the flower for which they are being made. Roll the paste firmly into position around the wire (the wires rarely need gluing into place).

2 Slightly open buds can be marked with a scalpel. When dusted, this marking will show quite strongly.

3 Buds for fleshy flowers need a stronger marking. Shape the bud and cut a cross through the top with scissors. Lightly squeeze these cuts back together and twist if required.

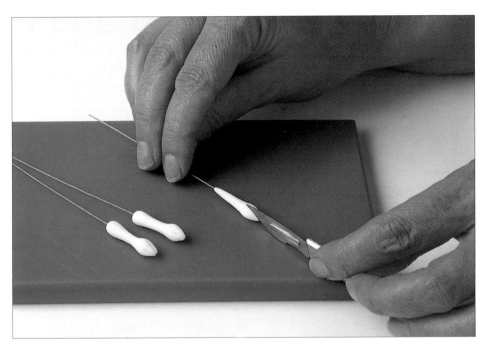

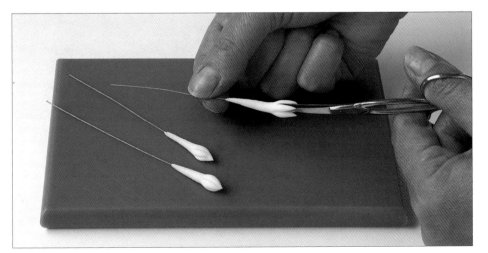

EXPERT ADVICE

Remember that buds are unopened flowers, so they should be similar in length to the petals of the actual flower. Tightly shut buds should be coloured green; buds that are just beginning to open can be a darker shade of the flower colour. Add calyxes to buds as well as to open flowers.

ARRANGING SUGAR FLOWERS

Just as real flowers can be arranged in a variety of ways, sugar flowers can be wired together in posies, sprays and bouquets for decorating cakes or making attractive table centrepieces. Remember, though, that sugar flowers are not as forgiving as fresh flowers. If they just knock together they are likely to chip or break rather than ease each other into position. To help prevent this, strengthen the stems with heavier wires, thus making the flowers less likely to swing into one another.

POSY

For this traditional arrangement, flowers are taped together in a circular form with a domed centre. Start with the largest flower in the centre and add to this, gradually turning the posy round, making sure that you add flowers and leaves evenly. Ribbon loops (page 110) can be incorporated if desired.

The Victorian posy is built up in a similar way, but the flowers in each 'row' are always the same. For example, start with a rose in the cen-tre, then surround with a circle of primroses, then a circle of violets, and so on, finishing with a circle of leaves and a posy frill.

RETURN

The return is a very small wired arrangement usually used as a supplementary decoration on large cakes, perhaps made up in matching pairs or fours. The return is mainly used for building more complicated flower arrangements.

The aim is to achieve an overall triangular shape. Start with buds or the smallest flowers at the point of the return, taping them together with ¼- or ⅓-width florists' tape to keep the stems light and slim. Work your way up, adding to and widening the shape to achieve a triangle. As you add flowers, trim away any unwanted wires, to keep the main stem slender, but taking care not to trim away too much as this might lessen the strength of the stems.

SPRAY

The spray illustrated is made from one return and one posy taped together. As you become more practised at arranging sugar flowers you will be able to wire up a complete spray in one piece.

3 Place the return into the gap in the posy and tape the two pieces tightly together with ½- or full-width tape. Bend the long spike on the return as required to help the two pieces fit together neatly.

4 Trim the taped spike to the required length, and tape over exposed wire ends as necessary. Gently rearrange and adjust the flowers to complete the spray.

1 Make the return from a selection of the total number of flowers and leaves made for the whole spray. Tape together neatly, leaving a long, neatly taped spike at the end.

2 Tape the posy flowers together, leaving a gap at one side.

KNIFE SPRAY

Use very small flowers for this, such as blossoms, jasmine, etc., and small leaves, as the flowers can easily get broken when the knife is used to cut the cake. Use ribbon loops with very long tails (page 110) to make an attractive and practical arrangement. If you wish to make a knife spray to accompany a wedding or celebration cake, ensure that all the sprays, on cake and knife, match.

CRESCENT

The crescent is assembled from two returns and a posy (page 106), with the two returns curving around towards each other. The centre is therefore thicker and will have the largest flower in the centre. This large flower should also be positioned slightly higher so that as the sides of the arrangement get narrower they also appear lower.

HOGARTH SPRAY

The Hogarth is made from two returns and a posy (page 106), this time with the two returns curving in opposite directions. If viewed from a different angle, the whole arrangement will resemble an 'S' shape.

This arrangement is ideally used in a vase or holder on the top tier of a wedding cake, or laid flat on a single-tier cake. The returns should be made slightly longer than those shown previously (pages 106 and 108) as you will need to bend them in an exaggerated fashion to achieve an attractive pair of curves. Make the two returns as a matching pair and it will be quick and easy to tape them together.

Ribbons

A ribbon makes a pretty addition to any cake or arrangement of sugar flowers. Bows can be used on cakes in combination with ribbon insertion techniques (page 32). Wired ribbon loops are useful for filling gaps and providing a neat finish to sprays and arrangements. The loops can help to cushion flowers and stop them breaking.

Bows

1 Make a loop in the end of a long length of ribbon (do not cut lengths before you start) and wrap the ribbon around.

2 Push the loop through and pull tight to make the bow.

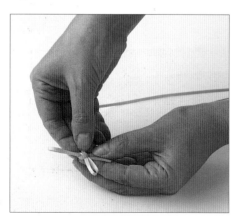

3 Pull the tails of the ribbon while holding the centre knot to adjust the length of the loops. Trim the tails to the required length.

Loops

TAILS Fold a length of ribbon in half, lay a 26-gauge wire on top of the fold and tape into place with ¼-width florists' tape.

DOUBLE LOOP (right) Make the first loop, fold the ribbon, make a second loop, fold the ribbon, and cut the tail to the length required. Tape to a 26-gauge wire.

OVERHAND LOOPS Wrap the ribbon around your fingers and thread a 28-gauge wire between your forefinger and the ribbon loops. Twist the wire tightly around the ribbon. Cut the ribbon tails to the length required. Tape the ribbon securely to the wire, pinching the ribbon at the join.

TULLE FLOUNCE Cut a square of tulle and fold in half and half again. Trim around the outside edge to create a circle. Tape the centre of the tulle to a 24-gauge wire, arranging the tulle as required.

EXPERT ADVICE

When using ribbons or tulle in flower arrangements, never allow them to overwhelm the flowers; they should only be used to fill and to provide background.

USING PICKS

Sugar is a preservative and besides being an attractive decoration for the cake underneath, it is there to protect it from bacteria and prevent it drying out. The wires used in making sugar flowers are not edible and should not be pushed into the cake through the surface of the sugar. Food-grade plastic picks are available which, when pushed into the cake, create a good seal as well as providing a holder for wired flower arrangements.

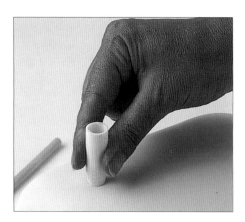

1 First mark the position for the pick with a pointed dowel, then push the pick into place, ensuring you leave a small amount of the pick visible above the surface of the cake.

2 Gently lower the flowers into position, cutting the taped wires

to the length required so that the arrangement sits neatly on the cake.

ARRANGING FLOWERS IN PASTE

Flowers don't always have to be wired into sprays; they can be arranged directly into flower paste, on or off cakes.

1 Make a small cone of flower paste and leave to crust for approximately 30 minutes. Cut the wires to the required lengths and push into the paste, holding each wire with tweezers. If doing this on a cake, first secure the cone of paste to the top or side of the cake with a little royal icing. When inserting the flowers, do ensure that the wires only go into the flower paste and

not through the sugar coating of the cake. If you are not practised at this, make the arrangement against a dummy cake glued to a cake board and remove to the final position when completely dry, securing with a little royal icing.

2 The finished arrangement can be used on a cake top or side, or can stand alone as a decoration.

GÂTEAUX

This chapter brings together everything required to make the most delicious gâteaux, including recipes for icings, frostings and coatings. Chocolate gâteaux are always popular, whether spread simply with buttercream or coated with a rich, smooth layer of ganache or pure chocolate. A section on chocolate techniques, including piping with chocolate and making chocolate cutouts and shapes, provides ample scope for the cake decorator.

ICINGS FOR GATEAUX

Unlike celebration cakes, gâteaux are usually coated in a soft icing, such as buttercream, fudge frosting, or even fresh whipped cream.

Glacé Icing

Glacé icing is very quick and easy to make, and, provided you work quickly, can produce attractive designs.

225g (8oz/1½ cups) icing (confectioners') sugar
6 teaspoons boiling water

Sift the icing sugar into a bowl and slowly stir in the boiling water until all the sugar is incorporated and the icing is smooth. Add colouring as required.

FEATHER ICING

1 Coat the top of a cake with boiled apricot glaze (page 13) and leave to set for approximately 5 minutes. Make up some glacé icing, take out 1 tablespoon, colour as required, and place in a greaseproof

paper piping bag. Put this to one side while you pour the rest of the icing (coloured if required) over the glazed surface of the cake.

2 Spread the icing over the surface of the cake with a palette knife.

3 Working very quickly, cut a small hole in the end of the piping bag and pipe a series of parallel lines

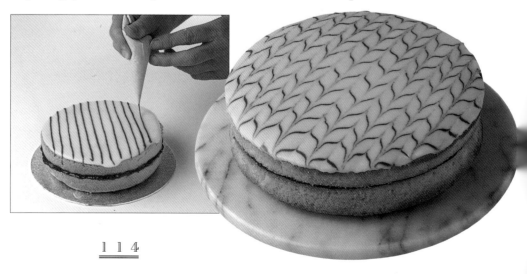

across the still soft surface of the coated cake.

4 Using the back of a pointed knife, quickly pull the tip of the knife through the soft icing in a series of lines at 90° to the piped lines. Repeat, making lines across the cake in the opposite direction, between the lines already scored. Leave to set.

5 When the icing has set, clean away any drips from the sides of the cake with a sharp knife.

Continental Buttercream

The sugar in this recipe is boiled (which changes the characteristics of the sugar), creating a very smooth cream which sets quite firm (particularly if the cake is refrigerated on completion). It keeps well because the raw egg is cooked when the boiling sugar is added. Follow the instructions carefully, paying particular attention to the temperatures – if you add the butter too soon the mixture will separate.

180ml (6½fl oz/¾ cup) water
620g (22oz/3 cups) granulated sugar
250g (9oz) egg
675g (1½lb) butter, softened

1 Place the water and then the sugar in a strong saucepan. Bring to the boil, washing the sides of the pan down to remove any sugar crystals. Do this with a clean pastry brush dipped in clean cold water.

2 Place a sugar thermometer in the liquid, and maintain the boil until the syrup reaches a temperature of 120°C (250°F). While the sugar boiling is progressing, place the egg in a large mixing bowl and whisk with an electric whisk until light and foamy.

3 When the sugar is ready, add it to the whisked egg, keeping the machine at high speed. Keep whisk-

ing at the same speed until the mixture in the bowl is cool. (You can, if you wish, wrap a clean tea-towel filled with ice cubes around the outside of the bowl to speed up the cooling process.)

4 When the mixture reaches blood temperature (test with your finger), gradually add the butter, whisking all the time until the buttercream is perfectly smooth. Flavour and colour as required.

FLAVOURINGS

Use flavourings as for Buttercream (right), but you will need to *treble* the quantities of flavourings for the amount of Continental Buttercream made in the above recipe.

Buttercream

100g (4oz/½ cup) butter, softened
175g (6oz/1 cup) icing (confectioners') sugar

Beat the softened butter in a bowl with a wooden spoon, or in a mixer. Gradually add the icing sugar, beating after each addition, until you reach a light, fluffy cream. Flavour and colour as required (see below).

FLAVOURINGS

ALMOND Add 2 tablespoons chopped toasted almonds and a few drops of almond essence.

CHOCOLATE Stir in 50g (2oz) plain chocolate, melted.

COFFEE Stir in 2 teaspoons coffee essence, or 2 teaspoons instant coffee mixed with 2 teaspoons hot water.

LIQUEUR Add 3 teaspoons of your favourite liqueur.

ORANGE Add 2 tablespoons fresh orange juice and the grated zest of one orange.

LEMON Add the juice and grated zest of half a lemon.

VANILLA Add 1 teaspoon vanilla essence.

Buttercream Gâteaux

Buttercream is often used to coat and/or fill Victoria sandwich or Genoese cakes, giving a deliciously rich taste.

1 Fill the cake with buttercream or jam (or both), and place on a cake board. Mask the top and sides of the cake by smoothing on a thin layer of buttercream with a palette knife. This will stop any crumbs falling off the cake or mixing with the smooth finish of the buttercream surface. Chill the cake in the refrigerator for about 15 minutes or until the buttercream is firm to the touch.

2 Apply a second coat of buttercream, making it thicker than the first layer. Use a palette knife and a paddling action (see royal icing coating techniques, page 51) to layer the cream on. Smooth to a clean finish, ensuring the sides of the gâteau are perpendicular and the top flat.

3 To create a different finish, the top can be textured with a comb scraper. Place the cake on a turntable. Hold the scraper so that one end is positioned in the centre of the cake and the length of the comb is lightly pressed into the cream across the radius of the cake. Hold the comb in that position with one hand as you turn the cake a full 360° with the other.

4 To neaten the outside edge of the gâteau, mask with roasted nibbed nuts. The sides of gâteaux are often completely coated from top to bottom with a textured finish, usually chosen to enhance the flavour and texture of the gâteau. Choose from chocolate vermicelli; grated or chopped chocolate; nibbed, flaked or chopped nuts (almonds, walnuts, hazelnuts).

SAM Gâteau

MATERIALS

*20cm (8 inch) Victoria sandwich cake
(page 9) or 2 layers of Genoese (page 10)
250g (8oz/1 cup) vanilla buttercream (page 115)
25cm (10 inch) round cake drum
Apricot glaze (page 13)
75g (3oz/ ¾ cup) roasted nibbed almonds
75g (3oz) marzipan (almond paste)
Selection of food colourings*

EQUIPMENT

*Serrated icing comb
Teddy bear cutters (Cake Art)
Piping bag
No. 2 piping tube (tip)*

1 Fill the cake with buttercream and place on the cake drum. Spread the cake with apricot glaze, and coat with two layers of buttercream, as described on page 116. Press the nibbed nuts on to the side of the cake, brushing away any loose nuts from the board.

2 Colour the marzipan as required by kneading in a little paste colouring. Roll out and cut out the shapes (this cake design uses teddy bear character cutters). Assemble the shapes on a small board covered with clingfilm (plastic wrap). When firm to the touch, peel the bear off the clingfilm and position on the cake.

3 Colour a small amount of buttercream with paste or liquid colouring and pipe the letters of the name on the balloons with a no. 2 tube. Pipe the strings of the balloons in the same way.

CONTINENTAL BUTTERCREAM TORTEN

1 Use two different-coloured Victoria sandwich bases, and split each cake horizontally in half. Using a selection of plain round cutters, increasing in size, cut two of the layers into rings. Alternate the colours of the rings.

2 Layer the cake with a filling of continental buttercream, starting with a solid layer of cake, adding the layers of rings, and finally topping with the other solid layer. Place the cake on a board, and mask the whole surface of the cake with a thin layer of continental buttercream. Refrigerate to set.

3 Add a second, thicker, layer of buttercream, obtaining a smooth surface by placing the palette knife almost flat on the surface of the cake, with only a slight angle on the blade. Keep the blade angle as shallow as possible as this will give a smoother finish. Turn the turntable the full circumference until the surface is smooth, keeping the knife in the same position (see royal icing coating techniques, page 51).

4 Coat the sides of the cake and create a patterned finish with an icing comb.

5 The sides of a torte may be coated with chocolate vermicelli, grated chocolate or roasted nuts, etc. Support the torte with one hand under the board. Apply the coating with the other hand, allowing any loose coating to drop into the bowl below.

6 Torten are usually marked into portions. This can be done with a torten marker (a special piece of equipment, usually made from plastic, which marks round cakes into 12, 14 or 16 segments). Alternatively, use the back of a long knife. The marks should be made very lightly with very little pressure.

Chocolate and Mint Torte

MATERIALS

20cm (8 inch) chocolate Victoria sand-
wich cake (page 9)
20cm (8 inch) Victoria sandwich cake
flavoured with peppermint essence and
coloured with green food colouring
(page 9)
25cm (10 inch) cake board
½ quantity chocolate continental butter-
cream (page 115)
Chocolate vermicelli

EQUIPMENT

Plain round cutters
Icing comb
Torten marker, optional
Piping bag
No. 42 piping tube (tip)

1 Cut the cakes into rings and reassemble, layering and coating with continental buttercream as described in steps 1–4 on page 118. Coat the lower half of the cake sides with chocolate vermicelli (step 5, page 118). Mark the top of the cake into portions with a torten marker or knife (step 6, page 118).

2 Decorate the top of the cake as required, choosing a pattern for piping from the range shown. Note that the patterns shown are examples only; choose one pattern and repeat it in all the segments, or choose two patterns and alternate them. Decorate with sweets, if liked.

3 Chill the torten well before serving to ensure a neat, clean cut.

FONDANT

The main attraction of fondant is the smooth, glossy surface it gives to both large and small cakes.

Fondant

Fondant can be bought commercially but usually only in large quantities. This recipe gives a small amount and is easily made.

150ml (¼ pint/ ⅔ cup) water
450g (1lb/2 cups) granulated sugar
150ml (¼ pint/ ⅔ cup) liquid glucose

1 Using a strong, heavy-based saucepan (preferably copper), bring the water and sugar to the boil, stirring continuously with a spoon. When the mixture reaches boiling point and the sugar has dissolved, remove any scum from the surface with a metal spoon.

2 Wash down the sides of the pan with a clean pastry brush and water.

This will remove any crystals of undissolved sugar which, if left, can fall back into the mixture and start a premature – and unwanted – re-crystallization process. At this stage, whilst the mixture is still boiling, add the liquid glucose. Put a sugar thermometer in the syrup, and continue to boil until the mixture reaches 115°C (245°F).

3 Remove the pan from the heat. Lightly oil a clean, dry surface (preferably marble) and pour on the sugar solution. Leave to cool until the mixture reaches 35°C (98°F).

4 Agitate the solution by stirring quickly in circular or backwards and forwards movements with a wooden spoon, until the sugar becomes a firm, white mass. Use a plastic scraper to remove the fondant from the surface into a bowl. Cover with a very thin layer of water until required for use.

USING FONDANT

To achieve a smooth, glossy fondant coating, it is important to carefully control the temperature of the fondant during the warming process prior to coating. Should the fondant get too hot at this stage, the gloss will not be achieved and a greyish, dull coat will be produced instead. You will need to prepare some stock syrup to adjust the consistency of the fondant.

Stock Syrup

300ml (½ pint/1¼ cups) water
350g (12oz/1½ cups) granulated sugar

Place the water in a saucepan and add the sugar. Bring the mixture to the boil, stirring gently until all the sugar has dissolved. Leave to cool, then store in a clean jar with a tight-fitting lid. The stock syrup should be cold before use.

Fondant Fancies

MATERIALS
*15x10cm (6x4 inch) piece of Genoese
(page 10)
50g (2oz) marzipan (almond paste)
1 tablespoon Apricot glaze (page 13)
Fondant
Stock syrup*

EQUIPMENT
*Round metal cutter, optional
Sugar thermometer
Piping bag*

1 Prepare the Genoese as described on page 11, and coat with apricot glaze. Roll out a thin sheet

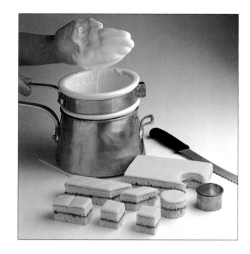

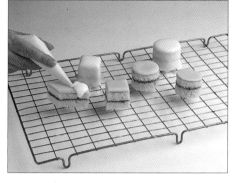

of marzipan and lower the glazed Genoese surface on to the marzipan. Trim away the excess marzipan with a sharp knife, and then cut the cake into the required shapes with a sharp serrated knife or metal cutters. Turn the cakes marzipan-side up.

Prepare the fondant by warming in a double boiler or bowl over a pan of hot water (*bain marie*) until blood temperature is reached (38°C/98.4°F). Adjust the consistency by adding small amounts of stock syrup; the consistency should be similar to that of double cream. To ensure the correct temperature is reached, stir the fondant during the warming process with your hand, and do not adjust the consistency until you have reached the correct temperature.

2 Place the prepared Genoese shapes on a wire rack. Pour the warmed fondant into a large piping bag and cut a hole (5mm/¼ inch diameter) in the end of the bag. Pipe the coating care-

fully over the Genoese pieces, ensuring that the sides are well coated. Leave on the rack until set.

3 When the fondant has set, remove the fancies from the rack by sliding a palette knife (which has been dipped in hot water) under the

base of each cake. Decorate as required (see below), and place in small paper cases or directly on to a serving plate.

DECORATIONS

To produce a variety of colours, first warm the fondant to the correct temperature and consistency. Coat some of the Genoese pieces with white fondant, then colour the fondant either pink or yellow and apply that. By adding orange at this stage you will obtain an apricot or peach colour. After that, by adding melted chocolate or liquid coffee, you can apply the darker shades. (Note that, when adding melted chocolate to the fondant, the consistency will thicken and you will need to add more stock syrup to bring the fondant back to a coating consistency.) Ensure the fondant temperature is kept at a constant blood heat (38°C/98.4°F). After the fondant coating has set, decorate with piped fondant and handmade or bought edible decorations.

GANACHE

Ganache is a rich mixture of cream and chocolate. It can be used in many ways: whipped as a filling or coating, or warmed for a pour-over coating. When set it can be used to fill chocolates. Delicious!

Ganache

150ml (¼ pint/ ⅔ cup) whipping cream
225g (8oz) plain chocolate, broken into small pieces

1 Put the cream in a saucepan and heat gently until boiling. Remove from the heat and pour over the chocolate. Stir until the chocolate has melted and has blended with the cream into a rich dark mixture. Pour into a clean bowl.

2 Allow the ganache to cool and set. It can be stored in this form until required. If refrigerated, ganache will keep for several weeks.

POURING GANACHE

If using ganache to pour over a cake, bring the set ganache to a pouring consistency by warming gently.

WHISKED GANACHE

Ganache can also be used for filling and piping on to cakes. The set ganache should be whipped in a mixer with a balloon whisk until light, fluffy and paler.

EXPERT ADVICE
Ganache should be at room temperature before whisking. If, once the ganache is whisked, it starts to curdle (possibly because the mixture was a little cool), add a knob of butter or margarine and whisk again.

USING GANACHE

1 Place some set ganache in the bowl of an electric mixer, and whisk with a balloon whisk until light, fluffy and paler. Use to fill and thinly coat the required cake base. Chill in the refrigerator.

2 Warm some set ganache in a bowl over hot water or on a low setting in the microwave. Place the chilled, coated cake on a wire rack. Pour the ganache over the cake and spread with a palette knife, making sure that the sides are coated. Lift the cake off the wire rack with the palette knife and place in position on a cake board. Leave to set in the refrigerator.

Chocolate Rose-Leaf Cake

MATERIALS
*20cm (8 inch) chocolate Victoria sand-
wich cake (page 9)*
Double quantity Ganache (page 122)
25cm (10 inch) cake board
*100g (4oz) plain chocolate, broken into
pieces*

EQUIPMENT
Piping bag
No. 13 piping tube (tip)
Fresh rose leaves
Small paintbrush

3 Remove from the refrigerator. Place some whisked ganache in a piping bag fitted with a no. 13 tube, and pipe a shell border at the base of the cake.

1 Fill and coat the chocolate cake with whisked ganache as described in steps 1–2 on page 122. Place on the cake board and pipe a border of whipped ganache around the base of the cake, as described in step 3, left.

2 Melt the plain chocolate in a bowl set over a pan of hot water. Clean the rose leaves with a damp cloth. Brush the melted chocolate over the shiny sides of the leaves with a small brush. Leave to set in the refrigerator. (A second coat might be necessary.)

3 Peel the chocolate leaves away from the fresh leaves, and arrange directly on top of the cake.

FUDGE FROSTING

This is a very rich, smooth frosting that is best enjoyed in the simplest way as a filling and coating for the Boiled Chocolate Cake (page 9).

Fudge Frosting

397g can condensed milk
100g (4oz) plain chocolate, broken into pieces

1 Place the unopened can of condensed milk in a saucepan of water and bring to the boil. Simmer for 2 hours, turning the can over after 1 hour. Make sure the pan does not boil dry. Remove from the heat and leave to cool. Ensure that the can is cold before opening it. Empty the milk into a clean bowl.

2 Melt the chocolate in a bowl over a pan of hot water, and stir into the cooked condensed milk. Stir the mixture well; it will be thick and glossy.

Chocolate Fudge Cake

20cm (8 inch) round Boiled Chocolate Cake (page 9)
25cm (10 inch) round cake board
Fudge frosting

Place the cake on the cake board. Spoon the fudge frosting on to the surface of the cake, and gently smooth it over the cake with a palette knife. Cover the whole cake in one application and decorate with a knife pattern (see below).

KNIFE PATTERNS

A variety of knife patterns can be used for this quick and simple cake:

1 Move the palette knife from one side of the cake to the other in a

shallow figure-of-eight motion, starting at the top (or side furthest from you) and finishing at the bottom (or side closest to you).

2 Using a small palette knife or table knife, make a figure-of-eight movement, firstly making a pattern down the centre of the cake and then on either side of the central one.

3 Place the cake on a turntable and the tip of a palette knife at the centre of the cake. Turn the turntable and gradually pull the knife away from the centre of the cake to the outside edge, making a spiral pattern in the frosting.

DAIRY CREAM

Cream is a popular gâteau ingredient. Whipped, it can be used for coating, filling and piping.

USING CREAM

Cream must always be used and stored at refrigerated temperature (0–4°C). Equipment should be clean and sterile to avoid contamination and possible food poisoning.

WHIPPING CREAM Place the cold cream (use whipping or double cream, or a mixture of the two) into a clean bowl and whisk to a peak, using a mixing machine, hand-held mixer or balloon whisk. Do not overwhisk (when the cream will start to go lumpy, yellow and have a greasy shine); stop whisking when the cream is still pale, but firm.

COATING WITH CREAM Spread the cream over the surface of the cake with a palette knife, using light strokes and taking care not to over-mix the cream at this stage.

Crystallized Rose Petal Gâteau

MATERIALS
Two 20cm (8 inch) round sponge cakes made using the Swiss Roll recipe (page 10)
100g (4oz/⅓ cup) best strawberry or raspberry jam
300ml (½ pint/1¼ cups) whipping cream, whipped
25cm (10 inch) round cake drum
50g (2oz/½ cup) roasted flaked almonds
Crystallized rose petals (below)

EQUIPMENT
Piping bag
No. 13 piping tube (tip)

1 Sandwich the cake layers together with the jam and a little cream, and place on the cake drum. Coat the whole surface of the cake with whipped cream, using a palette knife to achieve a smooth coat. Coat the sides completely with flaked almonds.

2 Pipe rosettes of cream evenly around the top outside edge of the gâteau using a no. 13 tube in a greaseproof bag or fabric bag with a tube adaptor.

3 Arrange the crystallized petals on top of the cake. Serve immediately or place in the refrigerator until required. Use this gâteau on the same day, whilst the cream is still fresh. Refrigeration for any length of time will destroy the crystallization on the rose petals.

CRYSTALLIZED PETALS

Many flower petals are edible, the most common being the rose.

When the petals have been encased in sugar and dried, they should be stored in an airtight container layered between sheets of kitchen paper. The taste and perfume when you bite into these will be as fresh as the day they were made!

1 Choose a good-quality, clean rose and carefully pull off all the petals, wiping them if required with clean fingertips. Paint over the whole surface of each petal with fresh egg white.

2 Drop each petal into a bowl of caster sugar and turn to coat completely. Dry on a wire rack.

CHOCOLATE

Chocolate is available in a variety of strengths and colours, the most common being plain (dark), milk (light) and white chocolate, as drops or in slab or bar form. Chocolate couverture (which contains cocoa butter and needs special handling) sets relatively hard with a high gloss, and is used for making chocolates or particularly delicate or fragile decorative pieces. Chocolate-flavoured coatings are easy to handle as they contain vegetable fat (shortening) and do not need 'tempering'. All the instructions in this section refer to chocolate-flavoured coatings.

MELTING CHOCOLATE-FLAVOURED COATINGS

Break the chocolate into pieces, and put in the top of a double boiler or into a heatproof bowl over a pan of hot water (*bain marie*). Heat gently, stirring occasionally, until the chocolate has melted. Alternatively, melt the chocolate on low power in a microwave, referring to individual microwave instructions for time and setting. Do not overheat the chocolate or it will become stiff, and will set with a dull, matte finish. To avoid overheating, do not allow the hot water to touch the bottom of the top pan or bowl containing the chocolate. Do not allow water to mix with the chocolate as this will also make it stiff and difficult to use.

COATING WITH CHOCOLATE

1 Mask the cake with a thin layer of chocolate buttercream (page 115) to ensure that there are no loose crumbs. Chill the cake briefly in the refrigerator, then place on a wire rack. Melt the chocolate as described left, and pour over the cake.

2 Smooth the melted chocolate over the cake, easing it over the edge and down the sides of the cake with a palette knife, making sure that all the sides are coated. To make sure that the chocolate is flat and even, lift one corner of the wire rack and tap gently on the surface below. Allow to set.

3 Melt a little chocolate of a different colour to the coating, and place in a small greaseproof piping bag. Cut a small hole (the size of a no. 1 tube/tip) and squeeze the bag to obtain a steady stream of chocolate. With a quick backwards and forwards movement over and beyond the edge of the cake, spin lines of chocolate over the surface.

Chocolate Roll Gâteau

MATERIALS

*15cm (6 inch) chocolate Victoria sand-
wich cake (page 9)*
Chocolate buttercream (page 115)
*225g (8oz) dark chocolate-flavoured
coating, broken into pieces*
*100g (4oz) light chocolate-flavoured
coating*
*25g (1oz) white chocolate-flavoured
coating*
20cm (8 inch) round cake drum

EQUIPMENT

Piping bags
Clean paint scraper
No. 13 piping tube (tip)

1 Fill and mask the cake with the buttercream and refrigerate the cake. Melt the dark chocolate and use to coat the cake as shown on page 126. Melt the light chocolate, place a little in a greaseproof bag, and cut a small hole in the tip. Spin lines of light chocolate over the whole surface of the cake (page 126).

2 Make a circular template the size of the top of the cake from a sheet of grease-proof paper, and cut in half. Place the two halves of the paper on the surface of the cake, leaving a gap of approximately 3cm (1½ inch-es) between them and lining up the straight edges of the paper with the lines of spun chocolate on the cake. Spin white chocolate over the exposed area so that the lines are at right angles to those underneath.

3 Make chocolate rolls as shown on page 129, and place on two opposite quarters of the cake, cutting to fit with a hot knife.

4 Carefully lift the cake with a palette knife and place on the cake drum. Pipe a shell border of chocolate buttercream on the base edge with a no. 13 tube.

EXPERT ADVICE

To cut the chocolate rolls, fill a tall jug with boiling water and stand the knife in it. Each time you cut, take the knife, now hot, and wipe it dry with a clean cloth. Make the cut and then return the knife to the water. This produces a very clean cut – and a clean knife.

Chocolate Decorations

Chocolate is very adaptable and can be used to make many different decorations which are simple, but delicious, and look attractive on all sorts of gâteaux and torten.

CHOCOLATE CUTOUTS

1 Melt the chocolate and pour on to a sheet of greaseproof paper. Spread out the chocolate with a palette knife.

2 Lift one edge of the paper and gently flick the paper, allowing the chocolate to spread further and encouraging the palette knife lines to disappear. Leave to set.

3 When the chocolate is set but not hard, cut out the required shapes using metal cutters.

4 Alternatively, to cut out shapes of your own choice, use a sharp knife with a rocking action for straight lines, or the tip of a sharp knife for curves.

5 When the shapes are firmly set, ease them away from the grease-proof paper by sliding a knife underneath. Lift them into the fin-ished position by lightly holding the sides of the shapes so that no fingermarks are left on the chocolate surface.

CHOCOLATE PIPING

1 To give greater control of mel-ted chocolate for piping designs, carefully stir in a few drops of glyc-erine. Allow time for the chocolate to react with the glycerine to create

the new consistency. This could take a few seconds.

2 Place the piping chocolate in a small greaseproof piping bag and cut a small hole (approximately the size of a no. 1 tube/tip) in its point. Pipe the required designs on to a sheet of greaseproof paper and leave to set. Chill if necessary.

3 Carefully ease each piece away from the paper using a palette knife, which can also be used to slide the piped decoration into position.

Using Chocolate Cutouts and Piping

Chocolate is a very versatile medium. The cake illustrated shows twelve different ideas for decorating torten using chocolate cutouts and piping. The cake is coated in orange buttercream, and grated chocolate (see below) is used to decorate the centre and base of the cake.

Grated Chocolate

Different textures of chocolate can be created by using a simple grater. Be careful to protect your fingertips when grating; use large blocks of chocolate, discarding the small ends which can be used for melting.

FINE SHRED This is achieved using the small blades on the grater; use for smaller cakes or coating the side of a gâteau as an alternative to chocolate vermicelli.

LARGE SHRED A heavier shred gives the chocolate the appearance of

small curls which can be used on larger gâteaux.

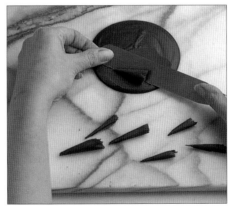

Chocolate Cones

Pour melted chocolate on to a work surface or marble slab, and leave to set. Holding the tip of a palette knife with your thumb, scrape across the surface of the chocolate in a circular movement, allowing the chocolate to curl naturally, in front of the knife, into a cone.

Chocolate Rolls

Pour melted chocolate on to a work surface or marble slab, and spread thinly and evenly with a palette knife. Leave until barely set. Cut the chocolate to the width of a clean paint scraper, then place the scraper at an angle of 45° to the chocolate. Push the scraper forwards, encouraging the chocolate to curl in front of the scraper. Trim the rolls to the required size with a hot knife (see Expert Advice on page 127).

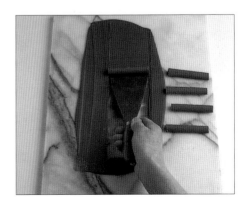

Chocolate Truffles

This recipe has been included to help use up cake trimmings. If you don't have enough trimmings, either save what you have in the freezer and collect more, or make a quick cake!

900g (2lb) sponge cake
trimmings
100g (4oz/ ⅓cup)
apricot jam
100g (4oz/ ½ cup)
Buttercream (page 115)
50ml (2fl oz/ ¼ cup) rum
(absolute minimum!)
400g (14oz) chocolate, melted
3–4 tablespoons chocolate vermicelli

1 Place the cake trimmings in the bowl of an electric mixer, and use a beater to break down to crumbs. With the machine still beating, add the jam, buttercream, rum and finally all but 3 tablespoons of the melted chocolate. You should achieve a firm mixture. If the mixture is soft, leave in a cool place for a few hours. When firm enough to handle, roll into small balls.

2 Roll the truffles in melted chocolate with your fingertips. Immediately drop the chocolate-coated balls into vermicelli, and roll in the vermicelli until well coated. Place on greaseproof paper to set.

EXPERT ADVICE

The truffle-making process is much easier with two pairs of hands – one dipping the balls in chocolate and the other coating them in vermicelli. Apply only a thin layer of chocolate to each truffle before dipping in vermicelli. Too much chocolate will distort the shape of the truffle or drip into the vermicelli, creating lumps.

ALTERNATIVE FINISHES

DIFFERENT-COLOURED CHOCOLATE Two coats, or even three for white chocolate, will be required for an attractive finish. For each coat, roll each truffle in melted chocolate with your fingertips, leaving to set between coats.

COCOA POWDER AND ICING (CONFECTIONERS') SUGAR Roll the truffle mixture into balls and drop directly into this powder mixture to coat.

ROASTED CHOPPED NUTS Roll the truffle mixture into balls and drop directly into roasted chopped nuts, turning to coat. Alternatively, mix the nuts with melted chocolate and coat using fingertips.

TEMPLATES

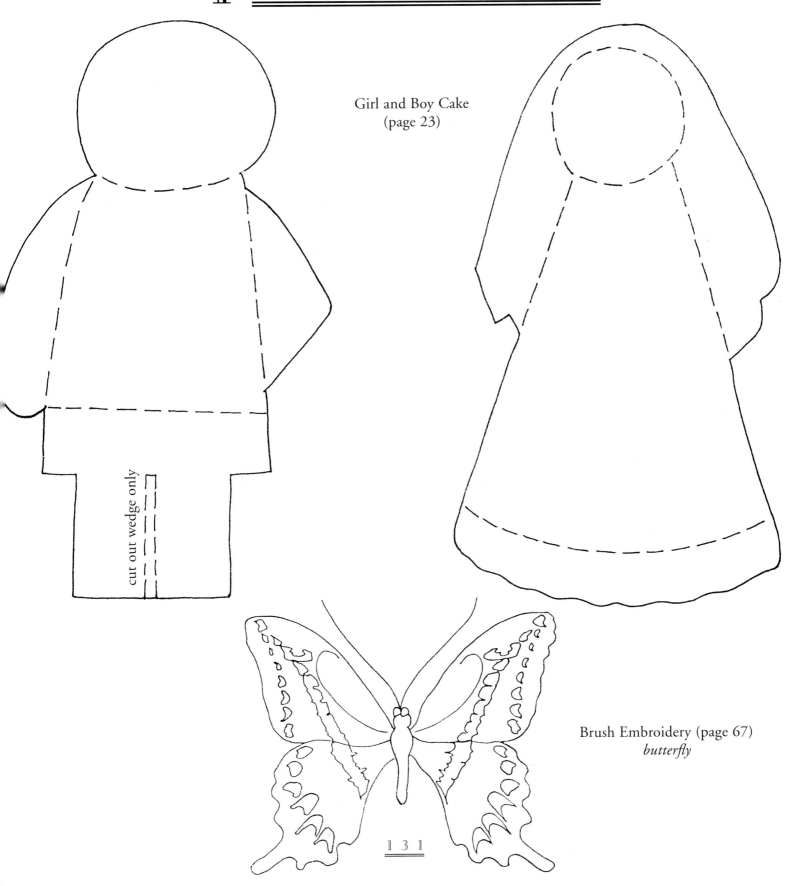

Girl and Boy Cake
(page 23)

cut out wedge only

Brush Embroidery (page 67)
butterfly

131

TIM Birthday
Cake
(page 30)

Pastillage Doves
(page 75)

Runout Dolphins
(page 73)

Tube Embroidery
(page 63)

side and board design

Rag Doll Cake
(page 44)

top design

Broderie Anglaise
(page 42)

practice pattern

Matchstick People
Cake
(page 48)

Direct Piping
(page 63)

fairy

Linework Template
(page 57)

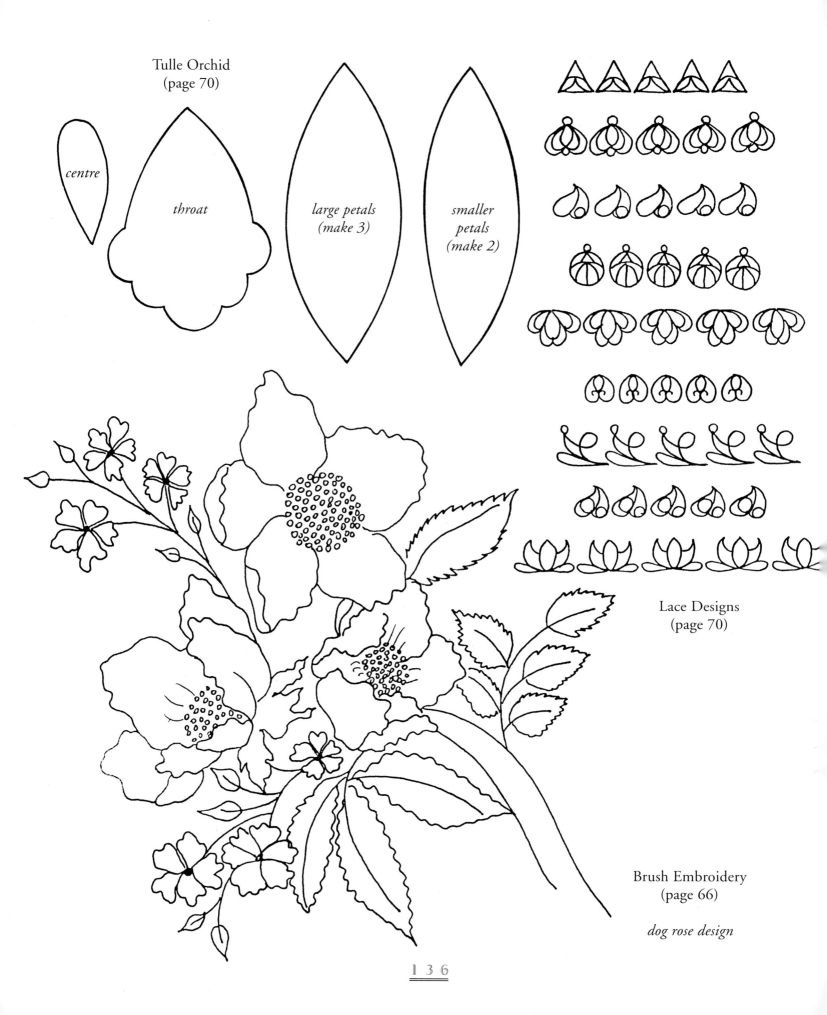

Tulle Orchid
(page 70)

centre

throat

*large petals
(make 3)*

*smaller
petals
(make 2)*

Lace Designs
(page 70)

Brush Embroidery
(page 66)

dog rose design

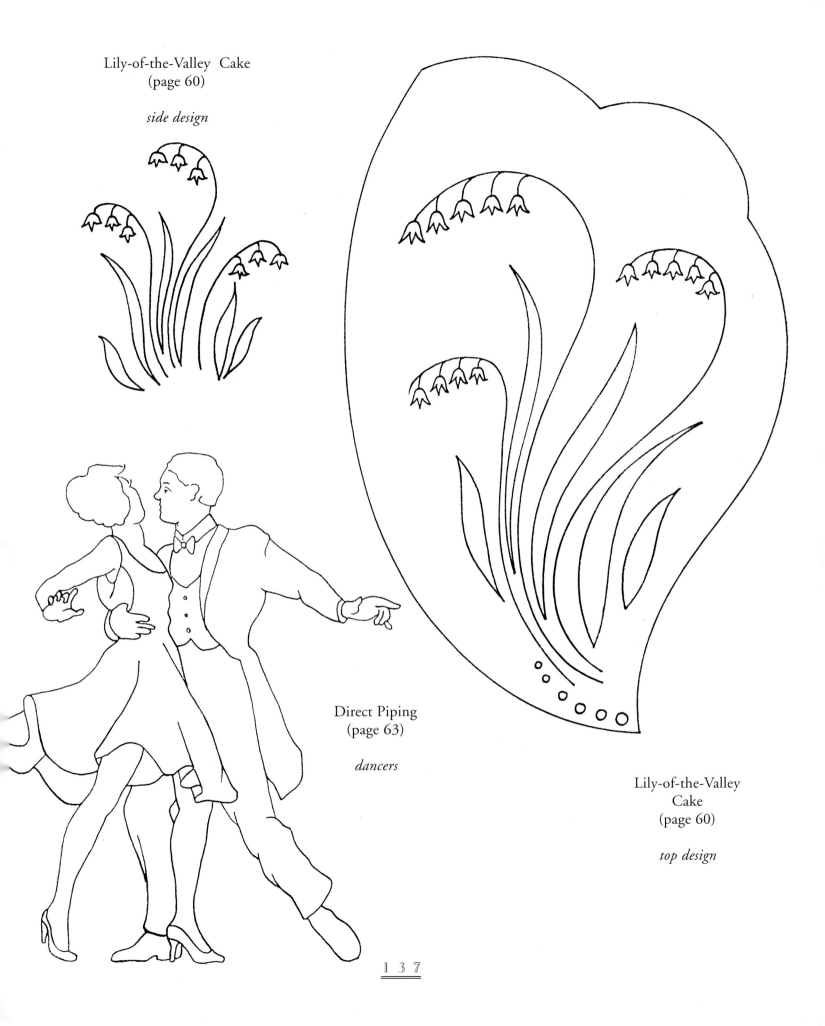

Lily-of-the-Valley Cake
(page 60)

side design

Direct Piping
(page 63)

dancers

Lily-of-the-Valley
Cake
(page 60)

top design

Wedding Cake
(page 64)

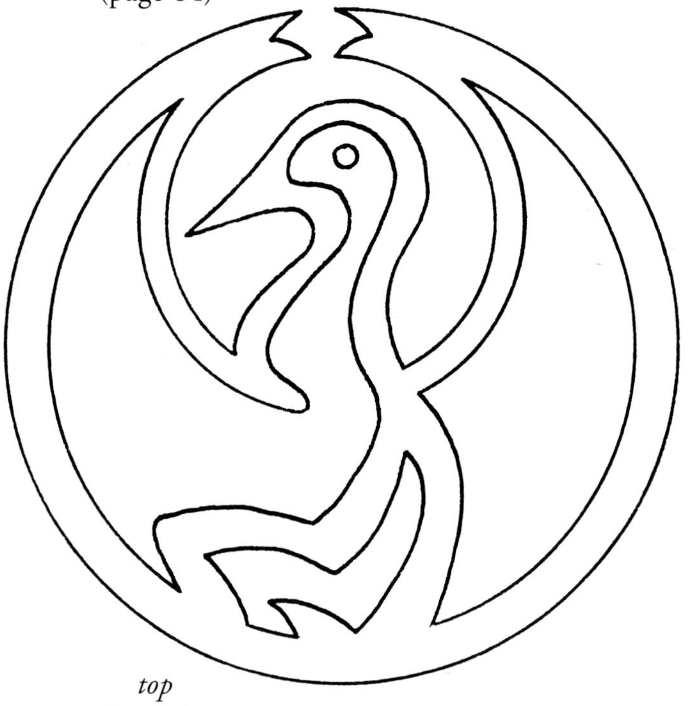

top decoration

Brush Embroidery
(page 67)

rose

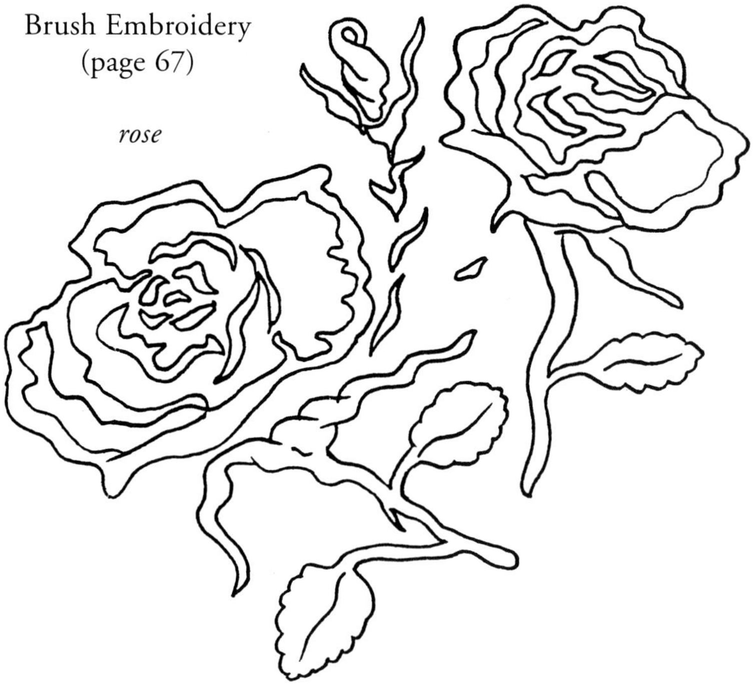

Fruit cake weight chart

Round Cake	15cm (6in)	18cm (7in)	20cm (8in)	23cm (9in)	25cm (10in)	28cm (11in)	30cm (12in)
Square Cake	13cm (5in)	15cm (6in)	18cm (7in)	20cm (8in)	23cm (9in)	25cm (10in)	28cm (11in)
Butter	125g /5oz/⅔ cup	150g /6oz/¾ cup	200g /8oz/1cup	275g/10oz/1¼cup	400g/1lb/4cups	475g/1¼lb/5 cups	625g/1¾lb/7cups
Soft dark brown sugar	110g/4½oz/¾ cup	125g/5oz/¾ cup	175g /7 oz/1cup	275g/10oz/1⅔cup	375g/15oz/2½cup	425g/1lb1oz/3cup	575g/1½lb/4cup
Glycerine	2 teaspoons	2 teaspoons	2 teaspoons	3 teaspoons	4 teaspoons	5 teaspoons	6 teaspoons
Black treacle	3 teaspoons	4 teaspoons	4 teaspoons	5 teaspoons	1½ tablespoons	2 tablespoons	2 tablespoons
Nougat paste-optional	2 teaspoons	2 teaspoons	2 teaspoons	3 teaspoons	4 teaspoons	5 teaspoons	6 teaspoons
Eggs	2-3	3	4	5	9	10	11
Plain flour	125g/5oz/1¼ cups	150g/6oz/1½ cups	200g/8oz/2cups	275g/10oz/2½ cup	400g/1lb/4cups	475g/1¼lb/5cups	700g/1¾lb/7cups
Mixed spice	1 teaspoon	1 teaspoon	2 teaspoons	3 teaspoons	4 teaspoons	5 teaspoons	6 teaspoons
Ground almonds	25g/1oz/¼ cup	25g/1oz/¼ cup	40g/1½ oz/½cup	40g/1½ oz/½ cup	40g/1½ oz/½ cup	50g/2oz/½cup	60g/2½ oz/⅔ cup
Raisins	100g/4oz/⅔ cup	150g/6oz/1cup	200g/8oz/1⅓ cups	250g/9oz/1½ cups	300g/12oz/2 cups	300g/12oz/2cups	400g/1lb/2⅔ cups
Currants	100g/4oz/⅔ cup	150g/6oz/1cup	200g/8oz/1⅓ cups	250g/9oz/1½ cups	300g/12oz/2 cups	300g/12oz/2cups	400g/1lb/2⅔ cups
Sultanas	300g/12oz/2cups	350g/14oz/1⅓ cups	400g/1lb/2⅔ cup	500g/1¼lb/3 cups	800g/2lb/5½ cups	1.2kg/3lb/8cups	1.5kg/3¾lb10cup
Glacé cherries	60g/2½ oz/½ cup	75g/3oz/⅔ cup	125g/5oz/1cup	200g/8oz/1⅓ cups	300g/12oz/2½ cup	400g/1lb/3cups	500g/1¼lb/4cups
Grated orange zest and juice	½ orange	½ orange	1 orange	1 orange	1½ oranges	2 oranges	2 oranges
Grated lemon zest and juice	½ lemon	½ lemon	1 lemon	1 lemon	1½ lemons	2 lemons	2 lemons
Rum or brandy for maturing	3 tablespoons	4 tablespoons	4 tablespoons	4 tablespoons	5 tablespoons	5 tablespoons	6 tablespoons
Baking time	1½–2 hours	2–2½ hours	3 hours	3½ hours	4½ hours	4½ hours	5 hours

Note: The metric and imperial measures in this chart are not equivalent. Use one set of measures only.

Wedding Cake
(page 64)

top loop templates

Brush Embroidery
(page 67)

oak leaves

Wedding Cake
(page 64)

lace

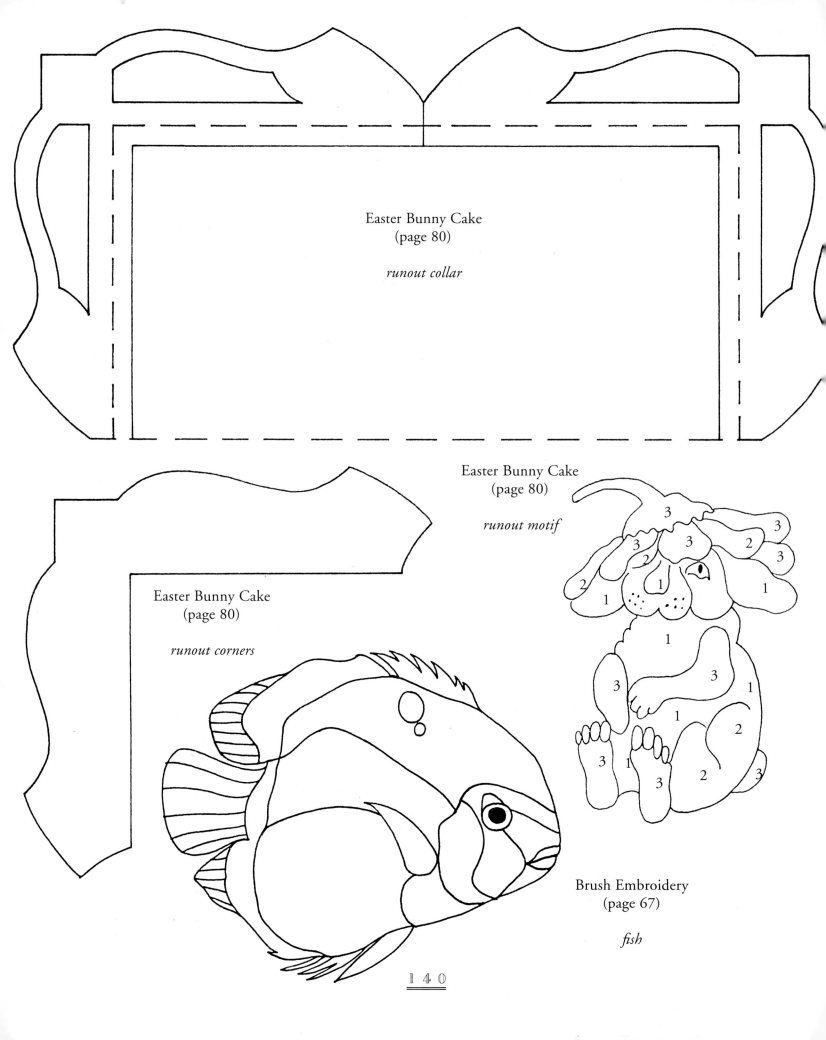

Easter Bunny Cake
(page 80)

runout collar

Easter Bunny Cake
(page 80)

runout motif

Easter Bunny Cake
(page 80)

runout corners

Brush Embroidery
(page 67)

fish

AABCDEEFG
HIJKLMNOPQ
RSTUVWXYZ

ABCDEFGHIJKLM
NOPQRSTUVWXYZ
abcdefghijklmn
opqrstuvwxyz

1234567890
1234567890
1234567890

1234567890

12345

67890

1234567890

1234567890

1234567

890

INDEX

ACKNOWLEDGEMENTS

Jackie and Chris would like to acknowledge, and express their thanks for, the technical genius, patience and fortitude demonstrated by Barbara, Helen and Anita in putting their quart into a pint pot! They would also like to thank the following suppliers:

CAKE ART LTD.
Venture Way,
Crown Estate,
Priorswood,
Taunton, Devon TA2 8DE
Tel: 01823 321532

SARAH GLEAVE CREATIVE STENCIL DESIGNS
Flanders Moss, Station Road,
Buchlyvie,
Sterlingshire, FK8 3NB
Tel: 01360 850389

J. F. RENSHAW LTD.
Crown Street,
Liverpool L8 7RF
Tel: 0151 706 8200

SUGAR CELEBRATIONS
176A Manchester Road,
Swindon,
Wilts. SN1 1TU
Tel: 01793 513549

SUGAR FLAIR
Brunel Road
Main Trading Estate
Benfleet, Essex SS7 4TS

The publishers would also like to thank the following:

GUY, PAUL AND CO. LTD.
Unit B4, Foundry Way,
Little End Road,
Eaton Socon, Cambs. PE19 3JH
Tel: 01480 472545

SQUIRES KITCHEN
Squires House,
3 Waverley Lane,
Farnham, Surrey GU9 8BB
Tel: 01252 711749

ANNIVERSARY HOUSE (CAKE DECORATIONS) LTD.
Unit 5, Elliott Road,
Roundways,
Bournemouth, Hants. BH11 8JJ
Tel: 01202 590222